THE T]

]

STEPHEN HORTHY
VICE-REGENT OF HUNGARY

Compiled by
THE WIDOW OF STEPHEN HORTHY
Edited by
LÁSZLÓ ANTAL
Translated by
ANNA NILSEN

THE TRAGIC DEATH OF

FLIGHT LT.
STEPHEN HORTHY
VICE-REGENT OF HUNGARY

THE WAR DIARY OF GYÖRGY FARKAS

THE ACCOUNTS OF EYE-WITNESSES

STEPHEN HORTHY REMEMBERED
BY HIS COLLEAGUES

PUBLISHED BY
THE WIDOW OF STEPHEN HORTHY

UNIVERSE PUBLISHING COMPANY

Original Title in Hungarian
HORTHY ISTVÁN REPÜLŐ FŐHADNAGY TRAGIKUS HALÁLA

Hungarian Book Publisher
AUKTOR KÖNYVKIADÓ, BUDAPEST, HUNGARY 1992

Complied and published by
THE WIDOW OF STEPHEN HORTHY
BORN COUNTESS ILONA EDELSHEIM-GYULAI,
MARRIED MRS. GUY BOWDEN

Hungarian book copyright
© Özv. HORTHY ISTVÁNNÉ (BORN COUNTESS EDELSHEIM-GYULAI)

Translator's copyright
© 1997, ILONA BOWDEN (BORN COUNTESS EDELSHEIM-GYULAI)

Translated by
ANNA NILSEN

All rights reserved. No part of this work covered
by the copyright hereon may be reproduced or copied
in any form or by any means – graphic, electronic,
or mechanical, including photocopying, recording, taping,
or information and retrieval systems without
written permission of the publisher and/or the author,
except by reviewers for the public press.

Library of Congress catalogue number: 99 096844
International Standard Book Number
(ISBN): 0-935484-19-1

Available from the Publisher:
Universe Publishing Company
185 W. Demarest Avenue
Englewood, N. J. 07631-2239 USA
Telephone: 201/567-4296
Fax: 201/567-6488

Printed in Hungary
Published in the United States of America

Flight Lt. Vitéz Stephen Horthy de Nagybánya.
From the collection of the widow of Stephen Horthy.

This English translation
of the original Hungarian Edition
I dedicate

to my beloved five grandchildren:
LEONARD-ISTVÁN, HELENA-LINDA,
HENRY, MANUELA and STEWART

and to my nine great grandchildren:
LOREN, GARRETT, DEXTER, MATTEA,
ROSABEL, LAILANI, RHYLAND,
HARLEY and BERENICE.

ILONA BOWDEN, WIDOW OF STEPHEN HORTHY

I particularly wish to thank:
ANNA NILSEN
for her excellent translation,
LÁSZLÓ ANTAL,
without whom the original edition would not have happened,
MÁRIA HOLLÁN
for her dedicated help,
MARIO D. FENYO,
who was participating to a certain extent in the edition,
and last but not least
GEORGE RÉDEY
for making publication possible.

ILONA BOWDEN, WIDOW OF STEPHEN HORTHY

Photographs by courtesy
OF THE WIDOW OF STEPHEN HORTHY
GYÖRGY FARKAS,

The photograph archive
of the Hadtörténelmi Múzeum
(Military History Museum)

The photograph collection
of the Legújabbkori Történeti Múzeum
(Museum of Recent History)

Contemporary documents by
courtesy of GYÖRGY FARKAS
and the Hadtörténelmi Levéltár
(Military History Archives)

Reproductions by
ATTILA KOVÁCS and LÁSZLÓ PINTÉR

IT MUST BE TOLD

As the fiftieth anniversary of my husband István (Stephen) Horthy's tragic death approaches, there is a continual stream of articles, reminiscences, and debates about the fatal flying accident. In Canada, the serial *Magyar Szárnyak* [Hungarian Wings] had published in 1978 a compilation of the research data then available: more recently, in 1989, László Bujtás published in Budapest a thick volume entitled *Hogyan történt? 1942. augusztus 20, 5 óra 7 perc. Horthy István repülő főhadnagy és kora eltérő megközelítésben* [How did it happen? 20th August 1942, 0507 hours—Flight Lt. Stephen Horthy and his times: a different approach], which deals mainly with this subject. But I might also mention Tivadar Ortutay's memoirs, *Két világháború sodrában* [In the maelstrom of two world wars], in which the author—Stephen Horthy's aide-de-camp and personal interpreter on the Eastern front—gives a detailed account of the tragic event.

When something out of the ordinary happens to someone famous, it is almost inevitable that there will be no end to the conjectures, each new version trying to outdo the last in its efforts to "explain" the event.

I would just like to refer to one or two circumstances which deserve consideration if we intend to arrive at an objective assessment of the possible causes of the accident.

When, on February 19, 1942, the Hungarian Parliament elected my husband Vice-Regent by acclamation, good wishes and congratulations poured in from Hungary and abroad. Only one of our "allies" remained silent: the German Third Reich, Hitler's Nazi Germany. Yet the sarcastic language propaganda minister Joseph Goebbels uses to describe the ceremony in his diary is well known. My father-in-law, the Regent, provides an account of it in his memoirs (*Memoirs,* New York: Robert Speller and Sons, 1957).

Another eloquent record of the opinion held by leading Nazis about Stephen Horthy may be found in a long report written on February 23, 1942, by Dietrich von Jagow, the German ambassador in Budapest. Drawing mainly on extreme right-wing and Arrow Cross (Hungarian right-wing, fascist-type party) sources, it described my husband as a most evil person, emphasizing that he was pro-British and anti-Nazi, and especially that he was not above befriending Jews. One of the accusations against him is that, as deputy managing director of MÁVAG (Hungarian State Iron, Steel, and Machine Works), he had prevented the implementation of certain German business ventures. Thus Germany could expect nothing but trouble from him in the future.

As we know, my husband volunteered to go out to the Eastern front, so that by serving in the military—he was a flight lieutenant in the reserves—he could get to know the actual war conditions and eventually make use of his experiences in politics. A few days before his tragic death I had the opportunity to spend some time with him in Kiev, where I was serving as a nurse with the field hospital. To our surprise we were accommodated in the luxurious villa of General Kitzinger, the German military commander of Ukraine. Apart from the staff and Gyuri, the valet, we were the only ones staying there. During our three days together we discussed everything quite openly. Naturally, we had a lot to talk about after such a long separation; moreover, my father-in-law had entrusted me with several messages to pass to my husband, one of which was that he must return to Hungary as soon as possible. I still cannot understand how we could have been so careless, or rather so unsuspicious, that we did not reckon with the possibility that the walls had "ears" (I found out subsequently that the house was, indeed, "bugged"). The point is that during those three days my husband told me everything he wanted his father to know and, in addition, he told me his secret plan. His experiences at the front had confirmed his conviction that the Germans had lost the war; furthermore, he was well aware that he could not change the country's predicament either from the front or from back home. So he had decided that, upon his return, he would find his way to England or the United States and try to do something for his country from there. But—he said—we, the family, must not know about this, so he would give us no details, lest it render his father's position even more difficult. We could denounce him as a traitor if there was no other solution. But he insisted that it was no longer possible to help Hungary from within, particularly as there were still too many people, especially among the military leaders, who believed the Germans would win. He also mentioned that, fortunately, he had not received any kind of decoration from the Germans. (The reader can imagine how I felt during the funeral service in the Parliament building when I caught sight of two high German medals among the decorations placed in front of the bier. They had been brought by Joachim von Ribbentrop, the foreign minister, "for the hero who fell in our common cause.")

It is not far-fetched to imagine that if the Nazi German leadership got wind of the tenor of our conversations, it would try its hardest to get Stephen Horthy, this inconvenient individual, out of the way as soon as possible.

But let me now return to the plane-crash which, according to several commentators, was caused by pilot error. In Kiev we talked a lot about Stephen's flights. As can be seen from György Farkas's diary, he had won his first dogfight by then and had also been involved in an incident where by chance (or was it really chance?) he found himself confronting German rather than Russian crews. I was always very interested in flying myself: after all, we had covered many thousands of kilometres together, and he had taught me how to fly. He was my teacher both at home and during the eventful flights of our honeymoon, when we flew across Italy, North Africa, Israel (Palestine), Syria, Turkey and Bulgaria in his Arado two-seater, without a radio or blind flying instruments. Two days before his accident he told me about the unfortunate tendency of the Italian Hawk (Héja) planes to "slip down" when making a turn. This had actually happened to him, but fortunately at an altitude of 4,000 metres, so he was able to pull the plane out of its slide. He was so focused and circumspect as a pilot that it is inconceivable that he would make the same mistake two days later at low altitude.

I have always had the feeling that the circumstances surrounding the crash were not investigated as thoroughly as they should have been. Reading Gyuri's diary reinforces this feeling. The remains of the aircraft were hurriedly packed up and removed; the accounts of the eye-witnesses are replete with uncertainties and contradictions.

Inevitably, the suspicion arose that Stephen's plane had been sabotaged by the Nazis. This was countered at the time with the argument that the Germans had no access to the Hungarian planes. It is clear, however, from Gyuri's diary, as well as from contemporary photographs, that there were Germans present at the airfield, and it was only normal that nobody thought of protecting the aircraft from them. Thus it is impossible to eliminate the possibility of Nazi sabotage.

The most despicable of the false rumours spread at the time was the accusation that Stephen Horthy was drunk when he took off, as he had been celebrating his name-day (the feast of Saint Stephen) the evening before, with Hungarian and German fellow-officers. This rumour was spread mainly by the Nazis and Arrow-Cross members. Quite apart from the fact that his valet's diary unequivocally refutes this charge, I myself can assert that I never once saw my husband drunk in all the time I knew him. He was abstemious in both eating and drinking.

After so many decades it is with understandable excitement that I leafed through the pages of the handwritten diary of György Farkas, in which he recorded day by day what was happening at the front. Judging by his tone and his descriptions, by the style of his narrative, I am completely convinced that every word is true. He records the events of the time with such accuracy (adding some details from memory), and brings my husband to life so faithfully, that I can almost see the events he describes with my own eyes, as if they had happened but today or yesterday. He portrays my husband exactly as I knew him.

My family and I owe him a debt of gratitude for this rare gift, the existence of which we did not even suspect. We also express our thanks to those others whose belated testimony has enabled us to get closer to the truth.

Ilona, the widow of Stephen Horthy,
Cascais, Portugal, May 1992.

György Farkas:
WAR DIARY
5TH JUNE 1942–21ST AUGUST 1942

The text of the following journal was translated from its original Hungarian. Translator and editor notes are featured in brackets and are written in italic form. Geographical places (in USSR, in Poland, in Romania) are referenced by their contemporary names.

5th June 1942 (Friday)
7:30 a.m.: departure from the main station in Szolnok. Said goodbye to Szidike [*György Farkas' wife*], who had come from Kenderes, and to my master. My luggage was placed in an ambulance carriage, where we are also going to sleep, which is pretty good. Three of us will sleep in one carriage.

Lunch at 12:30 at Újpest, then wrote a few lines to Szidike and to my family. Our army post office number is 245/23. Managed to get a few glasses of beer too, then it was time to leave. Spent the afternoon playing cards for cigarettes: won 50 Honvéds. The scenery was beautiful, but at Nagymaros we were lined up and warned, because it turned out that someone had been left behind at Újpest. Went to bed in the carriage at 9:30 p.m., the train carried on towards Érsekújvár [*Nove Zamky, Slovakia*] and the Slovak border.

6th June (Saturday)
Woke and washed at 5 a.m., got dressed; we travelled on in an orderly and disciplined manner. Our route was up the Vág valley, which was beautiful, but we needed two engines because one wasn't strong enough. Reached the former Hungarian border, the last major station was Zsolna [*Zilina*]. Then at the border station the Germans were taking a locked trainload of Jews to set them free somewhere. We sorry for the unfortunate souls. Our route through the Carpathians was very pretty, and by

6–7 p.m. we were going through occupied Polish territory. Towards evening we got to Oderberg [*Bohumin*], from where the Germans took us on quickly; went to bed at Katowice, it must have been about 9:30 p.m.. Lot of fortifications along the route.

7th June (Sunday)
Woke early in the morning because I was cold. Got dressed quickly at 4:30 a.m. and went back to bed. Then at the next place I washed down to the waist in really cold water. Here in Poland our progress is very slow and laborious. Every time the train stops, loads of children besiege it, asking for Hungarian bread and cigarettes. Sad, plaintive children's voices ask for "Hungarian little bread" by the train. On the way we've already seen barbed wire defences and shell holes left from 1939, houses blown to bits, and every so often a mass grave. Progress is terribly slow, every 10 km the train stops, sometimes as long as half an hour.

Still we get to Radom by 6 p.m. and to Deblin by 8: the only way we can go from here is to Kiev. The biggest Polish fortifications can be seen here on the banks of the Vistula and along the road. At 9 p.m. we left Deblin for Lukow, where we arrived in the middle of the night. The last station on the Russian–Polish border is Brest-Litovsk [*Brest, Byelarus*].

8th June (Monday)
Arrive in Brest-Litovsk at 5:30 a.m. and have breakfast here. The water's very bad and suspected to contain typhoid, so instead of water the Germans give us coffee, which is only coffee-flavoured sweet water, but tastes quite good cold. Along the way we see more graves— few of them; a few tanks, and overturned and burned trucks. Empty Hungarian trains rattle past us on their way back.

Arrive in Snitowo, where we are given lunch at 1:45 p.m., then set off soon afterwards. By 2:30 we are in Janow [*Ivanovo, Byelarus*], where we meet the Nagyatád border guards coming from Pécs. A longer rest here, it's getting towards evening when we set off again. Arrive in Pinsk at 5 p.m. and in Luninets at 7. Here we had a short rest and preparations, and were warned to beware of gangs of snipers. Between Pinsk and Luninets there was a Soviet airfield with the wreckage of about 25 planes, but more than 200 had already been cleared away.

9th June (Tuesday)
(Rokitno marshes)

Partisans attacked the train during the night, but without success; there are bullet-marks on a few carriages. I slept so soundly that I didn't notice anything. Everyone's got so used to the great noise here.

We're going through the middle of the Pripet marshes. There are loads of large mosquitoes. At one of the intermediate stations we met the pilots from Kolozsvár. We were stopped here all day because gangs of partisans had taken up the rails ahead of us. The Nagyatád troops went on the length of 15 carriages without the railway but then regretted it because they spent the whole day putting them back on. Andris Takács [*György Farkas' brother in law*] went through here too, but we could only exchange a brief greeting.

10th June (Wednesday)
Set off again around 7 p.m.. No sign of war. To our great surprise we saw 3 carriages (one an officers' carriage) and 3 trucks of the Nagyatád troops' train derailed on the right of the track. Luckily the only casualty was a broken arm, nothing else. The next obstacle was a Hungarian train which had been on its way back empty and

blown up: a load of wrecked trucks. Towards evening the intimidated locals were ordered out to guard the track so we could go on.

11th June (Thursday)
Arrived in Gomel at 6 a.m.. Rested here because German trains were racing through. There's a Hungarian station HQ here as well. Sent two letters from here. Set off for Bryansk at 12; during the night we couldn't go because of the partisans, so we didn't get there until 7:30 a.m.. All the blown up bridges and trains on the way aren't interesting any more. The infantrymen from Debrecen were in Bryansk.

12th June (Friday)
Got to Bryansk at 7:30 a.m.; breakfast; short rest. Although this is the eighth day of the journey, I feel completely rested. Bryansk is a sorry sight: not a single intact house to be seen, everything is in ruins. On the way, about 30–40 km before Orel, we had our first air raid, which was nothing special. There were 7 bombers, they dropped their bombs in the forest, far from the railway. The German fighters set off in hot pursuit and shot at them. They only managed to strike right next to the railway in one place. Lunch in Orel, loads of railway carriages here too. The station is just a few walls here and there. Not many houses have roofs. About 40,000 of a population of 140,000 are here, the rest have fled. Spent the whole afternoon here; at 10:45 p.m. the Russians launched a bombing raid until 11:30, but missed the station by miles. The intercepting fire was like a firework display. Then at midnight we set off for Kursk. Thought a lot about home during the night, slept badly.

13th June (Saturday)
Early in the morning we were already on the outskirts of Kursk. A quick breakfast, then unpacked. Everything's fine, the only big problem is that my boots are rubbing my heels, I can't wait to get to the airfield and take them off. 12 noon: set off from the railway to the airfield, a distance of 54 km. The road is dreadful, several times I thought we would overturn; but the traffic is worse than on the Rákóczi Street in Budapest. Got to the airfield in the evening, and set up camp in a forest, for one night to start with. The real fireworks started in the night. They haven't discovered us yet. The big problem is that there isn't enough water even for drinking, but vipers are plentiful. There are military polices here too, who will provide guards, and in particular eliminate the partisan gangs, which are plentiful, and well armed. But the policemen interrogate them in true police fashion, and the end is always the same, they just have to dig their own graves first.

14th June (Sunday)
Reveille at 5 a.m., unfortunately can't wash; morning parade, various orders. Prayers. Pitched tents. The sappers are building a fairly decent wooden cabin for my master. Spend the whole morning putting compresses on my heels to make them heal up. Meanwhile I get hold of a flask of water to wash and shave. The afternoon is spent doing the same and reading. In the evening I moved across to the finished tent, where there are 19 others already. The other officers' servants are here too. Would have liked to watch the nightly firework display, but found it impossible to stay awake.

15th June (Monday)
Reveille, then the same boring morning as usual. I sleep well all night, but this morning I had a sleep out in

the sun which was sheer perfection. At 2 p.m. we went to bathe, but unfortunately the water was like a puddle, not suitable for bathing; so I did some washing and it was dry by evening.

16th June (Tuesday)
The weather's turned sad, but the atmosphere is still excellent. Can't go out of the tent much because it's raining cats and dogs. This is how we spend the whole day, though the cards are getting some wear and tear.

17th June (Wednesday)
Rain all day. A bit of ironing in the morning, then played cards solidly all day in the tent. Nothing happened all day.

18th June (Thursday)
His Highness's birthday is a holiday even here. In the morning we had three cheers for the Regent. It just keeps on raining. It stopped later, but as it's a feast day we spend today playing cards too. A festive lunch at midday (tomato soup and pasta with cheese). Later in the afternoon we were given champagne and chocolates which, like all our food, cigarettes and cigars, we get from the Germans. I've got loads of cigarettes but not many Marks. I still haven't got my back pay. I get 8.20 Marks for 10 days, which is very little, but I'll still send it home because there's nothing much here to spend it on. Now I wish I'd sold all those cigarettes on the way, but I hope I'll still get a chance to sell them. From 5 p.m. onwards the others practice presenting arms while I sit under a tree trying to cure my bad foot. It doesn't stop me moving around, it's completely all right, but it keeps getting worse and painful towards evening, because the weather's turned worse too. In the evening the men tell stories in the camp, loads of laughter etc.

19th June (Friday)

It's two weeks today since we left Szolnok. There the weather's beautiful, but here the rain's dreadful, it's a punishment to set foot outside the tent. All we do is play cards, read, and sleep. The atmosphere is depressed. Lunch is bad. A bit of sunshine in the afternoon was a pleasant surprise. General Szabó [*Major General László Szabó, Vice-Regent Stephen Horthy's aide-de-camp and the head of his military office*] was here too. I also spoke to Captain Mátyás Szabó, and if the weather is suitable, we will go into Kursk. There I'll be able to meet people I know, because Harmath [*Ferenc Harmath, a staff sergeant in the Guards*] is there too. We can't wait for the planes to arrive, and I often wonder how His Highness is, how he's being looked after, etc. In the night I dreamt I was at home, it was so good I didn't want to wake up, though it was already 7 o'clock. My foot has really turned serious, though I didn't think it would. I got an injection because the whole leg swelled up. I thought it would kill me, and even started writing farewell letters, but it improved after the injection. They didn't put me on sentry duty although I would have liked to do it, because last night one of the soldiers hit a 2nd lieutenant who had drunk too much champagne and picked a quarrel with the sentries in the night. A stray bullet sent one of our anti-aircraft gunners to the next world. Nobody knew where it had come from. Anyone can be surprised like that here. Since we've been here the Russians have flown over us every night to bomb the nearby town of Kursk. We just enjoy the fireworks. We go to bed after midnight. The sun goes down at 7:30 here, by 9 it's pitch black. The forest is dark and quiet, we mustn't have any lights anywhere. The nights are cold, but we have two and even three blankets. Our beds aren't particularly comfortable: a bit of chaff on the ground, because there's no straw here, and if we slept on the green grass we'd just catch cold straight away. The small cushion is doing good service. The woman's touch can be seen here too, because those who are married, like me, have lots of things. And a little extra food from home is worth a lot too. I hope when my master is here, things will be better than they are now. There's no water at all for drinking, we drink tea or coffee, but it's dreadful, it's just about drinkable cold. It's true that we have that instead of water, but we have it for breakfast and supper too.

20th June (Saturday)

In the morning I went back to the doctor [*Captain Rátvai from Baja*], he gave me a good bandage, which was very good, the only problem is that the weather's horrible: wet and windy, and it's so cold that you can see your breath even in the early afternoon. We're warmly dressed and wear our coats in the tent; nobody wants to go out. All the orderlies who are here with me were on sentry duty last night and are sleeping huddled together, even their heads are covered. In the other corner a game of cards is well under way. The road's got much worse, they couldn't even bring water from the town, so there was no hot lunch, just some sausages. In the afternoon I tidied my clothes and polished my boots well and hung them up, I'm wearing the canvas shoes I've been given here. In the evening we had some impossible supper with no name: ground wheat, corn, peas, barley, and lots of other things—like a kind of thick pigswill with bran. [*Standard Russian army food: a mixed mush cooked in salted water.*] But we got some sweets afterwards to cheer us up. In the morning we always get synthetik honey, which is quite good. Later at night I felt sorry for the other orderlies and volunteered to guard the tent until midnight. It went very well. In my fur coat—in June—I wasn't cold. Had a long conversation with the supervising warrant officer and then looked at the beautiful starry Russian sky and the thick clouds passing over, which involuntarily made me think of home and wonder how my little wife was and what she was dreaming about. Slept deeply after midnight.

21st June (Sunday)
Beautiful sunshine, the only pity is that there's such a cold wind with it. As I'm still sick, I didn't go to the morning parade and prayers; I just said a prayer quietly on my own here in the tent, and asked the good Lord to help those at home, who must be thinking anxiously of me now as the bells peal for them to go to church. There's no church here and no bells, and no God in people's souls: just a desperate struggle for survival. Until now everything here belonged to the state, but now nobody even has anything to eat. It's very unusual to see a man anywhere. There are no men, just women and children, starving and worn down by suffering. We're about 25 kms. behind the front, and can clearly hear the artillery fire: perhaps preparing for the final reckoning with this terrible regime which has driven so many poor people into such ruin. We are still very well supplied, relatively speaking. In the afternoon the canteen was open too, with wine and other alcoholic drinks for the soldiers. In the evening we listened to Lajos Elek's stories: he makes the funniest comments.

22nd June (Monday)
A beautiful sunny morning, the wind's dropped, and my foot is much improved. I feel quite good. Wash one or two items, then lay myself out in the sun together with the clothes in a sheltered spot. However, the good weather has also given the Russians an opportunity, and this morning they visited us too—but they picked the wrong target and bombed the other side of the forest. Explosions rumble every 2 minutes, and planes come

over every half hour, but we don't let them bother us and get on with the washing, then hang our beautiful foot cloths out to dry. Later I looked at the wooden house which the sappers are building for His Highness here, it will even have a small garden. There are 4 rooms with proper floors, opening windows, and a balcony. We got our chocolate ration today. I'm going to take mine home: you can't get real chocolate there, and I think of my little wife in whatever ways I can.

23rd June (Tuesday)

Quickly dress, shave, and pack all His Highness's things. Leave for the town at 10 a.m. with Captain Szabó and the others. Got to Kursk after a long (4 hour) drive on the dreadful road. What a sorry sight the devastated town was can be seen from the attached pictures. [*The pictures are not included in this book.*] Not a single person is well dressed. The women wear clothes 15 years out of date, ragged and dirty. People drag two-wheeled carts along the roads, the woman pushing. Older children walk, holding on to their mother's skirt or the rope around their father's waist, younger ones sit on the cart in rags, crying. The whole procession moves on in lines stretching further than the eye can see, starving, ragged, blackened and grimy. On average 30 cars per minute go past them on the dusty road. In the town the Hungarian sappers have transformed a dilapidated house into a nice Hungarian-style one. There are 4 rooms, 1 office, 1 bedroom, 1 bathroom, and my room. In another, 3 rooms have been fitted out as an officers' mess. The rooms are in good order, painted, floored, everything. Water has to be carried into the bathroom and heated in the kitchen, but the drain works well. [*This house has been repaired for His Highness, this is where we will stay.*] I had lunch here today. We went to the post office as well, but no post has arrived yet. We went to the market, which is like the one on Teleki Square, but unbelievably dirty. Everything small—wheat, rye, flour, corn meal, bran, tobacco—is sold by the glass. Everything's terribly expensive, for instance Levente cigarettes are 30 fillers each. They sell milk and bread here too. The milk stinks from a long way off; the bread is black and rust-coloured. If anyone eats white bread, crowds gather around him as they would around a fatal car accident on the Rákóczi Road in Budapest. You can sell an army ration loaf for 13 marks (23 pengős). There's a lot of money, but for the locals there's no bread for weeks. Got back to the forest towards 5 p.m., had a second lunch. A bit of drill towards evening, then ceremonial burial of human waste, because a lot of men don't know how to behave. At night we sang songs as usual, then some wrestling, accompanied by much laughter. Stories, as usual, but no jokes: instead everyone tells a story from their own life. The best laugh is that of Lajos Elek who is 36–38 years old. He tells us about the old outlaws—he knew the last one, as he comes from Somogy county. Slept deeply after a long story session. The night was cold, though during the day it's pleasantly warm. We had nice sunshine and no wind, which is unusual here. But the planes fly directly over the forest all day, often touching the tops of the trees.

24th June (Wednesday)

In the morning after duties had been allocated I collected up my clothes and went with one of the groups to the lake next to the road to do the washing. The lake is about 5 km from the airfield. Washed and bathed from 9:30 till 11, then started back. We got back after a good hour's walk, refreshed and clean.

Back at the camp major cleaning and decorating work had been done. The boys made new beds, because up to now we'd slept on straw laid on the ground, which was cold and not too pleasant. Now our beds are higher, about

60 cm high, with plenty of nice soft straw. The area around the tent has also been laid out nicely, they've made flower-beds with various decorations. Everyone worked hard, and lunch tasted better for it. Rest period after lunch. It's worth mentioning that the Russian women who were also doing their washing in the lake were looking longingly at our soap: for them soap is just a distant memory. Their clothes just get wet, they don't get any cleaner than they were before. Some refugees were resting in the hollow next to the lake. I took two photos of them: they just stared at me as they ate their lunch. It had been cooked in a glazed earthenware pot, but smelt disgusting. It was a kind of mush, a Russian dish, its colour was like that of soaked bran, and it was thick, like a paste. They are dreadfully ragged, grimy and dusty, like wandering gypsies—perhaps even more so—though the refugees had seen better days. There were some among them who before Communism had been rich landowners, high-ranking officials, or indus-trialists. Here in the camp life is monotonous. We marked out the site of the tent for those coming by plane, we're going to put it up and sort it out as well as is possible here. The hunting lodge is progressing nicely, it might even be finished today. I think it will be better than the town house. If my master thinks so too, I'll bring a few things (cupboard, settee, table, chairs, bathtub, etc) from the town house. It will be nicely furnished. Today they caught another poisonous snake, quite short but dangerous: a common viper, with a cross marking on its head. We're expecting the planes any day. In the last few days we've seen lots of Hungarian planes around here, but the Russians haven't put in an appearance yet. Tonight, as it was fine and clear, they launched a huge bombing raid on the town, the road, and the railway, dropping at least 1000 bombs. Terrible barrage. With all the gunfire and bombs exploding the sky glows like at sunset. Even the trees tremble. Went to bed after midnight.

25th June (Thursday)

PT in the morning, which felt good, breakfast, then a noise like thunder. The Germans and Hungarians were together returning the Russians' visit last night. A huge number of planes went, loaded with packages. It was worth a bit to the Russians too, as tonight they only came in 3 or 4 planes. Nothing special happened, spent almost all day playing cards, though the weather's beautiful. Took part, as an expert, in the building of the officers' mess. Today was the first time I played 21 [*a card game black jack*]: first I won, then I lost 7 Marks. Marks are worthless here. You can only send your pay home, which isn't much, though some men have as much as 300 marks. The sappers are working very well, and the house looks beautiful. We can't wait for the post and the planes, because no post has come yet even though we've been here nearly 2 weeks. In the night I had a terrible nightmare: I dreamt that my master had died. Though I was at home, it was so dreadful I don't even like to think about it.

26th June (Friday)

The weather's beautiful. In the morning after duties had been allocated we had a medical. A few specimen insects of the slow-moving variety had put in an appearance. Several men had 1 or 2 lice. Who could have brought them to this far-flung forest wasn't easy to establish. It's possible that the captured Russian partisans who were brought to the camp brought them and left them here, together with their lives. It's also possible that soldiers who had been in the town had brought them back and spread them. I don't have any yet, and I hope it stays that way, as I'm about to move. General Szabó was here for lunch. I was called to the officers' mess and spoke with him. I think the arrival must be imminent, though I know things will only get worse, as then we can expect a significant visit from the Russians. I did very well at cards in the afternoon and again in the evening: I won 60 marks, which is equivalent to 90 pengős. I was very pleased, as I can send a good lot of money home as well—though superstition has it that if you win, that's when your wife cheats on you. It may be true, but I can't believe it—though I did have a disappointment and it felt dreadful. Tonight letters were distributed, the first lot since we've been here. I didn't get any, though there were loads. Some men got as many as 10. I was really sad, my heart ached.

27th June (Saturday)

Had a really bad night after not getting any letters, and at last morning came. After a bad night came a bad day. In the morning we had hard PT followed by a run. The captain was in a very bad mood too. It's true that the whole lot of us have got out of condition, all we've done is play cards, and nobody's paid any attention to anything, even himself. Several soldiers have got dirty and are infested with lice. There are some who haven't even changed their underwear since we set off—unfortunately there's one like that in our tent too. We were kept active all morning, without even a break for a cigarette. I suffered too, though I didn't have to, but I didn't want to be an exception. I had the floor of His Highness's room scrubbed, I just wish he'd come. In the afternoon a general de-lousing session, then at 5 p.m. PT again, and a meagre supper. After supper was our first opportunity to wash and shave. The others went to scrub the floors in the officers' rooms. No post today, so this has been the worst day since I've been here. Discipline! Quarrels and disagreements in the tent too, I can't wait to get out of here. And on top of all the bad things today, everyone still wanted to sing tonight. The only good thing to come out of this bad day is that they've put a stop to us playing cards, though I'm owed 46 Marks, and I've got 56 in hand (100 = 164 pengős)—I don't know when I'll be paid what I'm owed. There were two suspensions today as well [*a form of discipline in which the offender is suspended by his hands, which are tied behind his back, with his feet just off the ground*]—this is the first time I've seen it done, and it was dreadful even to watch. Two of the officers are called László, and as today is the feast of St László the officers had a very good party until 4 a.m.. They even had Hungarian gypsy music. Loads of champagne, brandy, everything (maybe they were drinking the men's rations). We can have some too, but I'm not prepared to pay 5 pengős for a beer—and then they only give you 200 ml. And I know that the men should be given that free.

There are German soldiers here with us, 5 of them, and they always get everything free when we have to pay a lot of money for it, and the Germans get their supplies at the same place and through our logistics. The captain had such a good time that he threw up. The Russians came in the night as well, I can't imagine what would have happened if by chance they'd attacked us. We wouldn't have got very far with our officers. There are lots of reasons why I wish His Highness was here already. I'm sure there wouldn't be such uncouth behaviour as there is now, even though soldiers are a loutish lot.

28th June (Sunday)

The first thing I did when I got up this morning was to iron 3 red white and green ribbons to decorate an altar. We should have had a camp mass today, but no priest came. After duties had been allocated I started carving furniture. I made 2 coat stands, 1 wash-stand, and 1 chair for my master's room. I couldn't make a table because the knife was rubbing my hand and giving me blisters. I worked at it all morning and all afternoon, like a caveman, because there are no tools and no materials.

Towards evening it even started raining, though there was a concert with units competing against each other. The prize for the winning unit was fish soup made with the fish caught during the day. There were nice songs as well as racy military pieces. It was a great laugh. The mechanics won first prize, the drivers were second, and we (headquarters and weapons unit) were third. The rest were a long way behind. The singing continued in the tent, though the general mood was one where you sing because you're sad or because you don't want silence. In their thoughts everyone, including me, was 1500 km away, at home. Occasionally there was an audible sigh. That night we found out that the Russians had shot down one of our reconnaissance planes, and one of our good old friends had burned to death in the plane, but not in Russian territory. Though already on fire, he came back home so that Hungarian soldiers could bury him and mark his grave with a cross. We also had some better news: 7 planes are coming on Tuesday, only I don't know if the person I'm expecting will be coming. I wish he would come, as I know he'll get fed up here and then we'll go home sooner. Everything's gone quiet, just the sound of breathing. I'm not asleep, and I know that several others are awake too, just not saying anything. At times like this you get dreadfully homesick, and it feels so unbearable you could die. Everyone thinks about their family, wife, children. Most of the men here are probably married. Though we aren't in any danger, the general atmosphere is really bad. The rain carries on falling persistently and quietly all night. Woke with a start towards morning: I'd dreamt that Szidike was terribly thin and ill. Felt dreadful and couldn't sleep a wink afterwards: terrible fears tormented me and I almost became feverish. This was the state I got up in next morning; and it just keeps on raining.

29th June (Monday)
Woke in a terrible state after sleeping badly. The weather's awful, just like the beginning of November at home. Today is the feast of Sts Peter and Paul, and there's thick fog here in the morning. As it gets light towards 8 a.m., it's still raining, and there's mud everywhere. No activities, we're all in the tent, nobody sets foot outside, we all just quietly tease each other: your wife's doing so-and-so now, etc. Feelings and thoughts are different for each individual, but equally bad for everyone. In the afternoon the sun came out. The ground dries up very quickly here. A short rest after lunch, then they called me out for a game of football. It was quite good, only I haven't run for a long time and got palpitations again. Had to concede that it's no use, I've got too old for this game. Sprained my foot and my left ankle: though it's not serious, it is a nuisance, especially now, because I've heard that the planes are on their way. I have to make a table this afternoon as well. I got hold of some boards, and the joiner made it up for 5 cigarettes: it turned out quite well. Towards evening all I could think of was whether my master is coming, whether he's bringing me any letters, and what he'll tell me about home. Here too, everyone's making preparations so that everything will be ready when the planes arrive. The evening is beautiful. Though playing cards is strictly forbidden, a pack does come out, if only very briefly. Won a few cigarettes.

The stories started up again tonight, but I felt worse that I've ever felt before. I can't rid myself of the conviction that something must have happened at home. For the first time I feel really jealous of my wife. It's true that I'm influenced by the awful things everyone's saying here about how the women at home are behaving while their husbands are fighting here and suffering the worst privation. Now I feel as if I could hang any woman who could do such things. Everyone here is faithful to his wife and family, though it's true that no civilian can get closer than 24 km to the camp. As to what the women here are like, all I can say is that a beggar at home is well-dressed and spotlessly clean compared to these. The night is short, as I couldn't sleep until after 2 a.m..

30th June (Tuesday)
Early in the morning I tidied up myself and my clothes. At 9 a.m. we had our first camp mass: it was moving and beautiful. Everyone, no matter how much he normally swears and swaggers, withdrew into himself and prayed together with the priest, for those at home as well. I don't know if those at home do the same for us even once. At the end of the mass it started raining again and we had to go into the tent. The rain stopped, I picked up the blankets and tent flaps, made curtains for the window, and tidied up my master's room. The rain was so heavy that the planes couldn't get here. The other officers' servants are assigned to sentry duty tomorrow, which means the planes probably won't come for another 2 days. Managed a bit of sleep in the afternoon. The weather's changed, it's nice and sunny now, though it's usually this changeable here nowadays. June here is like the end of April and beginning of May at home. In the afternoon some more card games, which ended with me losing a good bit; resolved not to play cards again. I don't know how long that will last. After 5 p.m. there was a bit of drill, but we just joked and laughed away from the others. At 6 the post was distributed; I was very upset that I still haven't received a letter. Unfortunately I can't even write any, as letter-writing has been banned for two weeks. We aren't allowed to ask for parcels either, because someone dared to ask his family to send him some bacon. I think he was right, because the food here is inadequate. For breakfast we get tea, but there's a load of sludge at the

bottom of it, and the same with the coffee. Lunch is a bad soup without any colour or taste, because there's no paprika and no onions. Then we get some kind of dried vegetable stew and about 50g of meat. Today, for instance, we had ground peas: it was like a corn meal mush. For supper there's bean soup, but it's just beans cooked in salted water: there's no roux to give it a bit of substance. Everyone's tightening his belt; we're on the 3rd or 4th extra hole. After supper there's a bit of compulsory singing: if the men are hungry, let them sing, then they'll forget they're hungry. Some of the men got parcels today. Then at night one or two stories, after which people go to bed with rumbling stomachs. Some drink a load of water to fill themselves up, but anyone who does that is up early in the morning, running as fast as he can to the latrine. If he's quick enough, he makes it; if not, he aborts on the way and then has to bury the result. That's the way things are here, but when the planes come everything's bound to change. Now all I want to know is when are we going home?!

SITUATION REPORT

Kursk is the nearest town to us; the Hungarian headquarters are there. It must have been quite a big town, because it had 500,000 inhabitants, about half as many as Budapest. The effects of Communism can be seen everywhere, because everything here belonged to the state, everyone just used things, nobody took care of or repaired anything. There are hardly any people in the town, and those who are here are terribly thin and ragged. More than half the houses are in ruins. This town has changed hands 3 times during the war. The women are filthy dirty, ragged, and all full of venereal diseases and the ubiquitous lice. Their dress... Their headscarf is generally a white rag which they drape around their head and neck and then tie. Their face is dirty, their eyes bleary; they stare blankly as a result of the venereal disease and of hunger. They wear a single dress, which is cut like a sack and made of a kind of dusty gray material, like working clothes at home. Some of them have a different kind of dress, made of rags. They have no stockings. Their shoes, if they have any, are odd: an overshoe on one foot and a white shoe or a boot on the other. Anyone who could has fled; those who are left have lost all hope. There are no fences here: they are unnecessary as everything belongs to one owner. There are some pavements, but only one concrete or tarmac road, the rest are muddy and full of potholes. There are no trams, but the traffic on the one road is so heavy that I counted 40 cars passing per minute. It's true that they're all military, mostly German. There are loads of soldiers: Germans, Hungarians, Italians, Slovaks, Latvians, Poles, and many others. You can't buy things in shops as there are only one or two shops, and they were distribution centres. The market is like the one on Teleki Square at home, only that's spotless compared to this one. Here you can buy pictures, cornflour, tobacco, rye, and all kinds of other small goods. The unit of measurement is the glass, and the currency cigarettes, marks, roubles, or bread. Bread is the most expensive, 1 kg of bread costs 32 pengős. There's a military cemetery here too. 250 Hungarians are buried in it, and many more Germans. The Russians bomb the town frequently even now. The airfield is 23 km south of this town, far from any inhabited area. No civilians are allowed in. We use a dirt track as there's no other road. Our camp is in a forest where there are lots more troops as well as us: police, sappers, and forced labour companies. The pilots from Kolozsvár and Ungvár are nearby too. There are anti-aircraft gunners as well. I'll describe the camp in more detail if I get time.

1st July (Wednesday)

The planes didn't arrive, the weather's good, nothing special happened during the day. The food was bad today and there wasn't enough of it. Some games in the evening; smartened up the officers' quarters during the day.

The night was beautiful. We're lying in the tent undressed, stories in full swing. Nobody bothers with the droning of the planes: we're all used to it. They drone over our heads every night, sometimes we can't even hear ourselves speak. Suddenly there's a whistling and swishing, the tent shakes, then an enormous explosion. In an instant everyone's in the trench. Then three more, smaller this time. Finally the parachute flare illuminated us. This was the first serious attack, and though the bombs fell 800 m away, it was still strange. Afterwards everyone went to bed and slept deeply. So ended an uneventful day.

2nd July (Thursday)

Today when duties were allocated we were given permission to write letters again. The armaments officer and a few others went out to find where the packages had fallen. They found them not far from the anti-aircraft gun. A big crater, and furrows radiating out around it where the splinters had been flung out. They brought a few pieces back. One piece could easily tear a man to shreds. A piece the size of my fist weighs as much as 700–800 g. It's completely split apart as if it were a piece of rag or paper. The weather's quite good; no activities; everyone tidies up his own area. They've already allocated men to guard duty for His Highness. [*The engineers have built the wooden hut, which consists of a single room. My tent is opposite the hut, 5 or 6 metres from the entrance: I can hear a call even if it isn't very loud.*] I've got hold of a lamp too, and everything's in perfect order. A telephone has been installed as well.

In the afternoon we were very surprised when Squadron Leader Csukás arrived [*Squadron Leader Kálmán Csukás of the general staff, commander of the 1st fighter division*]. His Highness and the others have landed at the nearest airfield, about 40 km away, and will only come here tomorrow morning. The front must be quite far away from here, but it's strange that we can hear gunfire all day. Last night Kursk had a major visit: by morning there were about 100 wounded and a few dead; quite a lot of both German and Hungarian casualties. The blast threw one man against a wall with such force that he practically disintegrated. The hospital is full to bursting: it was hit in the night, but only in one corner. Every day there are lots of mass burials, because large numbers of the defenceless Russian civilians die in each attack. The squadron leader went back to the reconnaissance base, where the other planes are, and they may still come tonight, or more likely tomorrow morning. Towards 8 p.m. Harmath and the others arrived. We carried in and unpacked the luggage. 2nd Lieutenant Ortutay [*Tivadar Ortutay, a reserve 2nd lieutenant in the infantry, the Vice-Regent's personal interpreter and one of the ADCs in his staff*] will spend the night here, the general won't come until tomorrow morning. To my great surprise it turned out that one of the drivers had been a schoolmate of mine in Baja. They were pleased to leave Kursk, as a bomb had hit quite close to them. The town is being bombed to pieces. They appeared here again tonight, but left us alone. The squadron leader didn't come back, and the planes didn't come either. At night we were on alert: until midnight we listened, fully dressed, to the Russians droning over our heads. Talked with Harmath about all sorts of things for a long time—until 1:30 a.m.. Time passes much more quickly than when you're with people you don't know. Wrote two cards today: one home, one to Kenderes.

3rd July (Friday)
THE PLANES HAVE ARRIVED! Quickly did the last bits of tidying up and unpacking in the morning. Harmath and the others have brought lots of nice things to eat and drink: we needed it too, because the food's very meagre here, and there's no water for drinking or washing. For breakfast and supper we get coffee or tea instead of water, but it's unbelievably bad. Photographers and the MFI [*Magyar Film Iroda—Hungarian Film Office*] are here, and journalists too. The arrival is expected at 3 today. The room looks nice, there's even a vase of flowers in it. The general is out too. Everyone here is very respectful to him, but he treats me like a good friend. The planes arrived at 2 p.m., with much rumbling and droning, but two of them were left behind at bad airfields on the way. Here too, one overturned while landing, luckily the pilot was small and wasn't injured. There were lots of photographers here too, and journalists as well. Everyone was very pleased, my master embraced me—he seemed pleased to see me again. He gave me the letters and parcels, which pleased me more than anything else, though one of the letters didn't contain much good news. Unpacked, and made things as comfortable as possible. [*In the afternoon we went in to the Hungarian headquarters in Kursk. Lodgings had been reserved for us here too, in a solitary house which even had a bathroom, though everything was in a very dilapidated state. Half the baggage was already in the house, and it was getting dark. We were standing there in front of the house with the car, when a sudden decision was made: my master decided that we wouldn't stay here but on the airfield in the little house.*] In the evening a good supper, there was even some champagne. From now on I'll get good food, because I'll eat in the officers' mess. The officers eat the same food as the men, but it's still better, and there's more of it. We talked a little in the evening, I

found out that everyone at home is well. Then, just as we were going to bed, red flares started flying around, indicating that the bombers had arrived. This is how the Russians work. Soon there were fire beacons near the airfield too [*—just like 200–300 years ago*]. A unit went out and was able to put out the smaller fire, but then a stack of straw was set alight, and they couldn't put that out. They came back late in the night. Fortunately the Russians left us to sleep in peace, they just carried on bombing Kursk relentlessly. In that night's raid the house in Kursk which had been repaired for His Highness got a direct hit. Even the communication trench in the small yard got a direct hit. It's lucky we hadn't occupied it: we'd have been killed on the very first night! The officers and those who arrived today are freezing here, they're all wearing leather jackets and use 3 or 4 blankets.

4th July (Saturday)
Reveille at 6 a.m.. His Highness got up quickly as well. Brought him hot water, he washed, shaved and got dressed. He only has linen clothes and is freezing: he's wearing all his warm clothes, but it's unseasonably cold here. He liked the breakfast too, though it wasn't particularly good.

Duties were allocated after breakfast, then he went out towards the front lines with General Szabó to reconnoitre the area. They came back quite soon, though it was a distance of 80 km. [*Major General László Szabó was formerly a military attaché in Rome. Now he's the Vice-Regent's military adviser and escort. His main duty in this post is to assist the Vice-Regent with advice in political and military matters and to ensure his physical safety. It's his job to make arrangements for travel and visits, to brief him on what to expect when he gets there, and to ensure his safety on such trips.*] Lunch after the flight. Then a short rest, and later briefing and planning. Made another shelf and two coat stands to give more storage space. Worked hard, because we made warm clothes and boots: it's warm clothes that are needed here. Managed to finish everything today. The weather's very strange: the sky is clear and it's pouring with rain.

In the night the Russians fly around overhead, but don't drop any bombs because they can't see anything to aim at. They do fire some flares, but far away, so they're looking for us well away from where we are. Now we can't stay here much longer, though it's comfortable enough now for us to spend the whole time here.

5th July (Sunday)
Got up early today too, just like any other day, because in wartime there's no such thing as Sundays or feast days. [*Reveille has been at 6 a.m. since the planes arrived.*] Did a big wash today, it didn't even occur to me that today is Sunday. Tidied up the linen clothes too, because this afternoon the officers and His Highness went into Kursk to pay formal visits to the Hungarian and German headquarters. Later in the afternoon they went to the theatre. Here we just stood by. There was only one short flight. Count Nándor Zichy was here for lunch: he's a soldier too and an old friend of my master. The weather's not wonderful. Nothing new or special happened. My master too was shocked by the squalor and dereliction here. They were back by 8 p.m., because at night you either can't go anywhere, or if you do have to go somewhere, you must do it in pitch darkness, without any lights, even by car. Supper was a very small piece of cheese, the cheese from home was very good: that's what filled us up.

6th July (Monday)
Ironed until noon, everything went smoothly. The pilots were awaiting the first sortie in a state of great

excitement. [*Four fighters went out escorting bombers, but nothing special happened.*] Everyone else rested after lunch. Suddenly the order came, and we're like an ants' nest that's been disturbed, everyone's working. In 2 hours even the tents had disappeared from over our heads. Everything was packed and loaded up, ready to move. We stayed overnight with a few officers, the rest set off at 2 a.m. for Tim. The loudspeaker truck plays music, all the nicest Hungarian marches and songs. There were four of us squashed into a small tent, lying like the pages in a book. In the night the Russians bombed the town again, successfully this time: towards 9:30 p.m. they hit a convoy of oil and fuel which was standing on the railway. We could see the flames and the black smoke from here, 20 km away. But they didn't come back later. Reveille at 1:30 a.m., everyone boards the trucks, and we're off. The trucks rumbled into life, and at 2:15 p.m. all 40 of them set off, leaving this comfortable and good camp. Staff sergeant Harmath and the others came back this afternoon from the front lines, where they were able to see the Russians fleeing in disarray. In one Russian armoured attack the Germans blew up 180 tanks with their new anti-tank gun, without suffering any losses. [*Or so they tell us here. (It reminds me of a first world war story in which the town crier lists how many prisoners we took on the Italian front by the Piave, and how many dead and wounded there were on the other side. An old peasant woman asks him: "Tell me, weren't any of our sons taken prisoner, or wounded, or killed?" He replies: "That's being announced by the Italian town crier on the other side.")*]

7th July (Tuesday)

This morning was the first time His Highness took part in a sortie. They were escorting bombers, and the raid was successful, but unfortunately they didn't encounter any enemy aircraft which they could engage in battle. The Russians only come at night, like owls, that's when they hoot. In the afternoon His Highness and I went down to the nearby lake to wash ourselves down a little. The water's terribly dirty but not very smelly. It's swarming with frogs and leeches. First His Highness went in and I stood guard in case someone surprised us. It was as much as he could do to throw off all the leeches. Then I went in, though I didn't fancy it much, because the water's very dirty. They attacked me too, I could hardly wash myself. We walked home, somewhat refreshed. On the way I noticed that we'd picked up some lice [*which was enough to make me check thoroughly and iron every item of clothing back at the camp*]. The distance was about 1 km.. At night we all went out to watch the Russians come and drop their bombs. The night was beautifully clear, we could see the town well from the hill. They throw out their flares, which have parachutes and stay in the air for a long time, making it as light as day. In this illumination they throw out bombs like mad. The town is a heap of ruins, the people walk around like nervous wrecks during the day, and at night they stand in the streets in desperation, nobody dares stay indoors. Here over the airfield the smoke from a volley looked like parachutists descending. Within minutes everyone was armed and ready for the order, when it became clear that it was only the smoke from gunfire. At 11:30 p.m. they dropped a flare over our heads. We went to bed in the illumination, which made it as light as day.

8th July (Wednesday)

The squadron leader Kálmán Csukás stood by until 5 a.m. waiting for a reported enemy reconnaissance plane, but it didn't come. No sooner had he come in and got undressed than it arrived and started taking photos of us. We're so popular, even the Russians come to take photos of us. The morning was quiet, we spent it sunbathing; then lunch with the Kolozsvár troops, who are still here and will set off tonight for Tim. In the afternoon the squadron leader came with us to the lake but didn't bathe because he didn't want to go in the dirty water. As we got back the order to stand by for a sortie was awaiting us. His Highness was the first to be ready. They left at 6 p.m., escorting bombers. They went in towards Vladivostok [!] and dropped their bombs, but didn't encounter a single enemy plane. Night was falling fast, it was already dusk, 8:15, and the planes still weren't back. Anxiously I went out to the landing strip. On the way, to my great surprise, I saw Mr Bezuk the director in a car—I was sorry I couldn't speak to him. A few minutes later the Hawks droned in two by two. His Highness was the second to land: he misjudged it slightly and ran into the squadron leader's plane, but fortunately there was no damage. But the fifth plane with Pilot Officer Panczel didn't arrive. Its engine cut out, and he landed fairly near the airfield without his undercarriage. There was no major damage, just a bent propeller. The pilot officer started walking back and then got a lift in a German car. The breakdown truck went out with the doctor to look for him; they came back at 5 a.m. having found neither the plane nor him: instead they'd found a crashed Russian bomber. They came back in the morning tired and covered in mosquito-bites and nettle-stings, and were greeted by the well-rested pilot officer. A similar thing could have happened to the Vice-Regent's plane too; he could even have been forced to make an emergency landing in enemy territory...

9th July (Thursday)

The Kolozsvár section hasn't left, and we're staying too. The new airfield is unsatisfactory. The ground is unsuitable for landing, and there's no tree cover so we can't hide the planes. Our operational company is there already, but we're waiting so we can move a long way forward all at once, and go straight to a better place. The Kolozsvár people are feeding us now, and they're looking after us very well. There were three sorties today: there was an attack in the morning, then at 1:15 they took off again to escort the bombers. They came back safely after 2. A quick lunch and a short rest, then at 3 they were off again. The other group went as well, barely half an hour later. Squadron Leader Csukás was in the second group. On the way he mistook a German Ju-88 for a Russian plane and started firing at it. The German took the matter seriously and fired back so effectively that he shot through the butt of the machine-gun on the plane, and left several bullet-marks on the plane too. Then they recognised each other and ceased firing, luckily no harm was done. But today we received orders that we will after all have to move to a new airfield near Tim, where the land section has been for a few days already. The Kolozsvár men broke camp too and left early in the morning. I started packing too: I'm taking everything that can be moved, because the Botond can carry it. This truck came with Harmath and the others and is only used for transporting luggage. This is a very good and quite pretty place, the airfield is fairly good too. We've been all right here, except that there's no water suitable for bathing in, and now summer has arrived with a vengeance. We can sleep without blankets even at night now. The night will be short, because the Kolozsvár men will wake us early, they're giving out coffee at 4 a.m.

10th July (Friday)
The Kolozsvár men left at 6:30 a.m.. We gathered up our bags too, and left for the new airfield at 9:30. On the road we passed loads of horse-drawn carts—they

stretched over 20–30 km. The road is terribly dusty, a chimney-sweep is cleaner than we are. We look dreadful in the open truck. After Kursk we reach the line from which the offensive began. Graves, and shot up and burnt out trucks. Dangerous mines over a large area still, though the army have collected loads already. The smell of corpses and carcasses: dead horses and cows which have stood on mines are everywhere around, but it's impossible for anyone to bury them as they might meet a similar fate. The road is dirt track all the way: it's dusty and full of potholes, with steep slopes in places, which the horse-drawn carts find a real struggle. We passed the Kolozsvár men before Tim, but it still took us all day to cover 132 km: we didn't arrive until 6:30 p.m.. The planes droned over us around noon. The airfield is very bad: it's full of potholes and it slopes. Even His Highness overturned on landing. As the plane runs along the ground, the engine drops and the tail is thrown forward. He was lucky this time: he had a near-miraculous escape. When a plane overturns, either it catches fire and burns out, or the pilot is crushed between the armour plate and the fuselage. The plane broke up. [*There was a full complement of service personnel at the airfield, who reached the overturned plane in their truck within minutes, and lifted the tail enough for the pilot, who was hanging upside down, strapped into his seat, to open the canopy and crawl out of the plane.*] There have hardly been any sorties and no dogfights so far, and already four planes are wrecked. The airfield is completely unsuitable for planes like this, though the forced labour company here has cut the grass and flattened the hummocks. In fact it was the fact that the grass had been cut which caused His Highness to overturn. We don't even have a tent, the Vice-Regent will spend the night in a shared tent. Here I unpacked the essentials and had a good wash. Hermann, the clerk and unit leader, made room in a small tent. The

Kolozsvár men were left behind on the bad road, so they didn't even arrive in the night. Our staff, who arrived a few days ago, already have quite a farm. There are 2 calves, 3 sheep, and a piano and hurdy-gurdy too. The music plays, the mosquitoes bite. Someone got septicaemia through a mosquito bite. Our men buried the corpses and carcasses here.

11th July (Saturday)
Had a good rest, only my dusty eyes have gone red. There's plenty of water, there's a lake nearby as well. No flying, so we go to bathe in a lake 7 km away, where there's a water mill. The water's not particularly clean, and there are plenty of leeches too. I couldn't do the washing here; I did it back at the camp after lunch. [*We took a machine gun with us, and I sat with it on the shore while the Vice-Regent bathed: I was bodyguard and sentry all in one; then we changed over while I bathed. Such was the security for Vice-Regent Stephen Horthy at the front, where partisans sprouted like weeds in the fields.*

Walking back, we see a man suspended from a tree at the edge of the camp: an aircraftman, who had been disciplined in this way by a 2nd lieutenant. This 2nd lieutenant was a reserve officer, in civilian life he was a teacher somewhere near Kispest. And the reason for the punishment? The aircraftman had been squatting in the grass, fiddling around with something. The 2nd lieutenant saw him in this position and shouted at him: "What do you think you're doing there? Are you s-------g by any chance?" The aircraftman stood up and responded properly, but with a touch of humour, to the strange question: "Things are very lean here, sir, there's nothing to s--t." The 2nd lieutenant flew into a rage at this response, as if stung by a wasp. "Two hours suspension!" He immediately arranged for the punishment to be carried out, and the aircraftman was suspended from a tree with his hands tied behind his back. Luckily the man hanging in a strange position didn't escape Flight Lt. Horthy's notice as we walked back. He got his knife out of his pocket and cut the rope, muttering "Unfortunate man"—that was all. The news spread like wildfire around the camp. This happened immediately before lunch; soon we were on our way to the table. The mess area was in the open, in the shade of some trees: tables were set for the officers here rather than in the tent. When the officers were all there and had sat down, Flight Lt. Horthy got up and said: "Gentlemen, on my way back to the camp I saw a soldier suspended from a tree. I cut the unfortunate man's rope. Gentlemen, I would prefer not to see this or similar disciplinary measures here at the front, please." The officers knew about the affair already and were casting sidelong glances at the 2nd lieutenant, who was also sitting at the table, eyes downcast. That was the end of the matter; it was edifying and extremely effective.] For lunch we had one of the calves, but these cooks don't cook very well. Shaved after lunch; Mr Jány [*General Gusztáv Jány, commander of the Hungarian 2nd Army*] is expected for supper. A chef couldn't have produced better dishes than mine: 1 plate of cheese, 1 of fish, 1 of crackers, 1 of bacon and salami. It looked nice and tasted good too: he didn't come, so we had to eat it all—though we had a bit to drink with it as well. It's hot day and night now, about 34° C during the day here in the forest. Anyone who can, bathes—other ranks included. The anti-aircraft gunners assigned to us went to bathe in the nearby lake too, though the water's fairly dirty. One unfortunate gunner had a heart attack in the water and drowned. The autopsy was carried out here and the cause of death was found to be a heart attack. He was buried at 7 p.m. by the road leading to the village of Stary Oskol. The town is about 9 km away. We are a long way east of Kursk now, about 100 km beyond it. Our troops are a long way beyond the river Don: the Russians are fleeing so fast they can't keep up with them. Our airfield is really bad, they can't fly sorties from here. His Highness is very upset that he hasn't got a plane and won't have one for some time, unless he flies in a borrowed plane. No particular incidents today. Not even the Russians disturb our sleep at night.

12th July (Sunday)

Got on with the ironing in the morning so I could have a bit of a rest at last. [*It's very hot, there are no flights because the overturned plane is waiting to be repaired. But there's another lake where bathing is possible; General Szabó and Flight Lt. Horthy drove there to bathe. They got back towards lunch time and Flight Lt. Horthy sat reading in a folding chair outside his tent. There was still a little time before lunch.*] At lunch time I always have to organise the officers' meal. The cooks wanted to kill the [*other*] calf today, but they couldn't find it anywhere this morning. It had been stolen. They set off looking for it—all they needed to do was follow the smell of cooking: the Kolozsvár men were in the middle of cooking our calf. So we have to eat mutton today. They'd bought the calf for money, it cost them 10 marks, and 1 sheep cost 100 cigarettes, or 1 pengő. [*The service unit always ate first, and so I usually had my lunch before His Highness. Today they made a meat hash with the fresh mutton and rice, since there was no veal. My tent was opposite His Highness's tent, about 5 or 6 metres away. I was sitting outside my tent eating my lunch. He saw that I was eating with relish, and asked me what there was for lunch and whether it was good. I replied that it was a rice and meat hash and that it tasted very good. "Could I have a taste of the men's lunch?" I remembered a recent conversation in which I'd told him that before the planes had arrived the food was very bad, and not only that, there wasn't enough of it either. Perhaps now that he saw me having my lunch he wondered just what the men were eating. I got the new mess-bowl which was still clean, packed in a bag together with cutlery. The kitchen was nearby, within 5 minutes I was back with the rice and meat hash. The cook looked surprised that I was back for more, but I told him I wanted a portion for Flight Lt. Horthy. Well, he gave me a portion all right: no fat on the meat, and more meat than rice. Flight Lt. Horthy ate with relish, and didn't even finish it all. Then he went to the officers' table and said: "Gentlemen, enjoy your meal; and thank you for lunch—I ate the same as the men, it was excellent, and there was plenty of it."*] With that he sat down at the table and chatted with the officers as if nothing had happened. But in fact something very important had happened: it wasn't difficult for the officers to realise that they didn't need to have separate catering from the men. So everyone benefited: there was no need to cook two lots of meals, and the general quality improved, because Flight Lt. Horthy was satisfied with what was provided for the men. Meals were still served in the officers' mess as before, but they weren't cooked separately any more. The day was uneventful and boring, we're waiting to move further into Russia. It's very hot here too. In the afternoon the mechanics came to repair my master's plane as quickly as possible.

Then he and the General went to bathe in another lake.

In the next village some Russian soldiers were captured: they'd been left behind and had hidden until now and were operating as partisans here. Hiding in a house, they'd shot dead a 2nd lieutenant who was at the front of the advancing Hungarian troops. The rest didn't fail to avenge the dead man: they rounded up the Russians and shot them. They captured and executed about 60 men. The Russians faced up to the rifles fearlessly, proudly pointing where they should aim. So the soldier fired and the partisan fell. This is how things are here in Russia. [*In wartime life is cheap.*]

13th July (Monday)
Mr Jány came today to visit His Highness. His Highness returned the visit at 5 p.m. in Stary Oskol, where we're moving tomorrow. There's a proper, good airfield there, and a good forest as well. The river Oskol is nearby too, we'll be able to bathe there. Went out to see how they were getting on with the repairs to the plane. The damage isn't great, it will be ready by Wednesday. Then the weapons people will calibrate the guns, and by Thursday it will be ready for action. The mechanics are working hard, though the food is meagre for men doing such work. His Highness gave them his extra ration and his bread. We haven't settled in for a long stay here. The terrain isn't good, and the whole place is wrong. Towards evening we found out that we were leaving in the morning. I packed some of the bags, and I'm ready to go.

14th July (Tuesday)
His Highness drove to the front with General Szabó to observe the front lines; and we loaded everything up and set off at 10 a.m. with the Botond and the Fiat car. On the way we were caught in a terrible rainstorm. The Fiat broke down and had to be towed. Water was flowing along the road, it was horribly muddy. We towed the car several times, until finally the whole bumper came off, just when we'd got to the worst stretch of road. It was sandy and full of potholes, only fit for jeeps. After much laborious toing and froing we got through, completely covered in mud. After that the road was a little better, there was even a paved section. We reached the forest, and unloaded the trucks at 5 p.m.. The tents hadn't been

put up yet, the forced labour company had just started doing it. My friend Sándor and I—[*Sándor Horváth, 2nd Lieutenant István Gyulai's batman, a lad from Szentágota, he survived the war and got back home*]—knocked up a small tent and I cut some fresh grass for it. His Highness and the others arrived just then and watched me scything and picking wild strawberries—there are loads of them here. But mosquitoes are more plentiful than anything else, and they're strange black ones. There's so much smoke you'd think the whole forest was on fire, but the mosquitoes are glad to see a bit of new flesh and are biting like mad. [*Just as well I brought the repellent, it'll come in very handy now.*] The tent's not ready but we could just about sleep in it. The planes arrived safely too, though 3 have been left behind for repairs.

15th July (Wednesday)

They finished putting up the tent this morning and I could tidy things away a little. At 10 a.m. a German general came to visit; His Highness received him. [*German soldiers come frequently, and signalmen work here too.*] Meanwhile, I went to demolish a nearby Russian repair workshop. It was a bit scary as everything here is liable to blow up. Still I got the roof off in an hour, though it was raining all the time. There was a good lot of boards and roofing felt. We needed 3 trucks to take all the boards etc back. Harmath and the others dismantled everything and built a nice little house with floors, windows, etc. His Highness went to collect his plane and returned in the afternoon. [*He brought the plane back, but the twin machine guns still have to be calibrated.*] It's hot here too. In the afternoon I went down to the river Oskol, which is really excellent, possibly even better than the Tisza back home. [*But the area is pretty dangerous, because there were Russian soldiers here very recently, and there was some fighting. There are still mines in the forest, and champagne bottles also explode when opened, causing burns.*] Bathing felt really good, as we'd worked very hard today: we've made a nice little wooden hut for ourselves too. Washed the vehicles and sank into the mud.

16th July (Thursday)
His Highness has flown his plane here. He's very pleased, though the guns still have to be calibrated today. This airfield is much better, there's a long and fairly wide surfaced runway, and the rest of the ground is cinders. There's also a quite a good hiding place for the planes at the edge of the forest. There are several wrecked Russian planes lying in the forest, but they've been completely dismantled. It's not advisable to walk through the forest, because everything's liable to explode. One soldier found a champagne bottle and pulled out the cork, but within moments his hands and feet were burned. The poor lad was a dreadful sight. Mines go off frequently here too. Tonight the Germans, who are close by, invited His Highness and General Szabó over. He stayed quite late, he got back at 1:45 a.m.. Nothing special happened.

17th July (Friday)
The planes are in perfect working order; His Highness got a new propeller in Kursk, because the one they'd straightened out wasn't perfect, and some new ones had just arrived there. Went down again to the Oskol to do the washing. It was very good. Got back at 2, because I'd made some morello cherry sauce with the signalmen who are on the river bank. The people live better and are a lot cleaner here. Their favourite flower here is the pelargonium, just as it is in Hungary. These are the Don valley Cossacks who sing so nicely, though the poor souls are pretty unhappy now. Around their houses the

gardens and fields are cultivated just like ours at home. They keep horses and cattle, and also pigs and sheep. If they spoke Hungarian they would be just like us, their customs and temperament are like ours. Poor Acting Pilot Officer Romer was unlucky again today. He was bringing the squadron leader's plane from the workshop where the bullet-holes had been repaired, but overturned badly on landing. The plane was completely wrecked. This is the third time this has happened to him. He got away with it again, he wasn't injured, but he probably won't fly again.

Tonight there was a sortie at the bend of the river Don, where the terrible giant Russian tanks are. [*The Russians defend strongly, they've concentrated strong armoured units here.*] The situation here is quite difficult, but things will soon improve, as the Stukas arrived today. Our men are getting ready to help the storm troops cross the Don tomorrow. In the evening we're told that reveille will be at 4:30 a.m., and the sortie involving all planes will take place at 3 a.m., together with the ground attack. [*Stephen Horthy was to join in this battle; the night before we discussed the arrangements for the next morning.*]

18th July (Saturday)

At 3 a.m. the engines roar into life: a terrible piece of music for the Russians. His Highness got up at 4:30 and looked over the preparations. I brought a little hot coffee, and he left at 6. The bombs fall out of the sky like rain; the Stukas visit the anti-aircraft defences. The Russians have started fleeing across the water by every possible means: on logs, rafts, ferries, whatever they can find.

The second group leaves at 8 a.m., because the visits are at 2 hour intervals. All kinds of bombs are dropping on the Russians, the new type of German bomb is particularly effective: it explodes with a dreadful noise. Squadron Leader [*Csukás*] attacked one of the ferries crossing the river, but was soon hit and quickly had to find a place to land. He put down in an area occupied by our forces, there was no major problem. Pilot Officer Panczel was watching and saw that he had landed safely; then he returned to base and took an Arado to pick up the squadron leader. They got back safely, no problems.

His Highness flew in the 3rd sortie at 5 p.m., and returned at 6:30. The Russians have had a visit they won't forget in a hurry. They've left everything behind, everyone fleeing as best he could. Tonight we had a film show here in the forest. The signals unit showed newsreels followed by a film, "Szücs Mara házassága" [*The Marriage of Mara Szücs*], which was very funny. Felt terrible, slept badly when I managed to sleep at all. The stewed mutton I'd had for lunch really did for me, I thought I wouldn't survive the night. I vomited until there was nothing more left, and got feverish too. Next morning I was like death warmed up. I think I'll never eat mutton again as long as I live. Major Tost arrived today too. [*Major Tost and Stephen Horthy were close friends and confidants: it was no accident that it was Major Tost who came to the front to give him a personal briefing.*] I was very pleased to get the letters and warm clothes, which will be very useful now. It's very cold at night.

19th July (Sunday)

His Highness went on a mission to secure the air-space over the bend of the river Don. No other significant incident. In the afternoon we went to bathe, Major Tost came with us. The radio people made recordings today, which will be broadcast at home, I don't know when. The camp cinema was playing again tonight: they were showing "A beszélő köntös" [*The Talking Mantle*].

20th July (Monday)
Today again there were a few missions to secure airspace and some bombing raids. The weather is beautiful. Major Tost went out again to look at the battlefield, where there are enormous numbers of Russian dead, with the dreadful summer stench which usually accompanies such events. Nothing particular happened: it's the period of calm which follows a big battle. They've reconnoitred the new airfield, we're waiting to move there. Packed Major Tost's bags as he's going home tomorrow. I'm lucky enough to be able to give him a load of sugar to take back home to Szidike, together with a long letter which nobody's had to censor.

21st July (Tuesday)
Major Tost left today, I gave him one more short letter. I sent home all the sugar and chocolate I'd collected up to now, I know Szidike will be pleased to get it. [*I wrote a separate letter describing our situation here. In my opinion the Vice-Regent is in great danger here. This letter is for Her Highness, I promised to keep her informed.*] The Russians left buried oil tanks here, but they're mined. After much effort the sappers got to them and found them empty. No flying; there was a lot of rain in the night, though that doesn't stop them taking off and landing, because the runway is concrete.

22nd July (Wednesday)
Nothing worth mentioning happened today; the weather's cloudy and unsuitable for flying. The Germans still shot down 23 planes. The land forces crossed the Don in a corridor 200 km wide.

23rd July (Thursday)
The first section left to move over to Nikolayevka. General Rákosi [*Lieutenant General Béla Rákosi, a plane*

spotter] was here for just under half an hour. No flights today. There was a film again tonight, they're entertaining us well. Tonight we saw "Behajtani tilos" [*No entry*] and "Életre ítéltek" [*Sentenced for life.*] [*The Vice-Regent read and chatted with the officers.*]

24th July (Friday)
After my usual morning jobs I went down to the river Oskol 2 km away to wash a few clothes and naturally to bathe. The commander of the air force was due to come for an inspection towards 10 a.m.. The inspection didn't happen because the commander's plane crash-landed. One of the engines cut out over the airfield and the undercarriage didn't come down, but they still managed to land safely. The land forces have advanced well beyond the Don in a corridor 200 km wide. 20 km away from here there's a valley which we've called Death Valley, because that's what it is. This is where the Germans used their newest bombs, which kill anyone within 4–5 km. Here in the valley there are loads of corpses and carcasses, thousands of them, but all the equipment is completely undamaged. There are no signs of injury on many of the corpses and carcasses: the fact that there are so many of them is due to the new bomb, and this is why we call the place Death Valley. They all look as if they've died a natural death—but we know that this German bomb is enormously loud when it explodes. Only those who are hit by the fragments have visible injuries; however, the bomb is filled with compressed air, which apparently destroys the lungs of anyone nearby when it explodes. This is all just talk and conjecture here, because they won't reveal the secret of the bomb; but there are definitely huge numbers of casualties who have been killed in this way. So they can get hold of loads of military equipment in completely sound and useable condition. No sorties today, just securing air-space and a bit of target prac-

tice. Tonight Lieutenant Colonel Pohly sent his gypsy musicians here, including some who are well-known in Budapest. We had a great time, we almost started dancing, they played so well. There are 24 of them, with a cimbalom and a double bass. The Russians don't come anywhere near us, it seems they're avoiding anywhere where there are fighters. The people are well off here, there are plenty of geese and hens. A loaf of bread is worth 1 goose or 100 cigarettes; 2 loaves are worth 5 geese. Lots of cooking everywhere. It's a shame we have to advance, because we've settled in quite well here, we've got used to the place. Some men go into the town to bathe in the pool, because the town is practically unscathed. The locals don't use it anyway, because they've moved out of the town.

25th July (Saturday)

No sorties or particular incidents today either; just a state of alert. Tonight the flying squadron brought us a pleasant surprise, because they gave us a good mess-tin of stewed goose to go with the rather modest supper, and naturally I got plenty of it as well. They couldn't have done better. Poultry's dirt cheap here.

26th July (Sunday)

His Highness went into the town early in the morning, at 7 a.m.. They were reconsecrating the church, which until now had served as a locksmith's workshop. There were loads of people at the consecration service, the Russians are very religious people. The church was completely filled with believers and others, as well as soldiers. As a sign of his respect, the Orthodox priest presented His Highness with a loaf of bread, some salt, and a nice little icon on a pretty dish, covered with a towel. The bread was excellent, made with butter, naturally he intended me to eat it, which pleased me, but then I shared it out. Here in Russia the holy bread is really excellent. They were very pleased that His Highness had honoured them by attending the service. [*General Szabó and 2nd Lieutenant Tivadar Ortutay, acting as interpreter, accompanied His Highness.*] No sorties or flights. In the afternoon we went bathing, at 6 p.m. there was a service in the camp. Tonight Baron Schell was here for supper; then they played cards and talked until 10:30 p.m..

27th July (Monday)
Nothing happened. In the afternoon His Highness cycled off to return the baron's visit. [*He went alone, with no escort: he knows no fear.*] They brought him back by car in the evening. [*One of the soldiers brought the bicycle back the next day.*]

28th July (Tuesday)
Nothing special happened. [*We've been preparing to travel for days. One section left here days ago to tidy up the new airfield.*]

29th July (Wednesday)
Got up at 4 a.m. protecting reconnaissance planes. Alert from 10:30, waiting for the Russian plane which appears very high up every day around this time. Whoever sees it first gets 5 pengős. Today it didn't come. However, reinforcements did arrive, consisting of 11 Hawk planes, 2 Arados and 2 Blockers. There's a good lot of planes here now. In the afternoon a little chat with those who have just arrived. Tonight the signalmen surprised us with another film show: "A férfi mind őrült" [*The Men Are All Mad*]. It was very interesting and funny, including the end of the show, because the wind got up and it started raining, so much so that the screen was blown off the top of the truck. By the time we got to our tents in the dark, we were all soaked to the skin.

30th July (Thursday)
Rain all night and all day. Flying was out of the question. There's terrible mud here as soon as it rains. On the road leading to the town there's a load of vehicles of all kinds which have skidded into the ditch or toppled over. His Highness still went into the town tonight: he and General Szabó had been invited to supper. It was nearly midnight when they got back on the muddy road in the dark.

31st July (Friday)
His Highness went on a sortie at 6:45 a.m.. They encountered Germans instead of Russians: luckily they soon recognised each other. The Germans came here for discussions, and it was agreed that from now on the Germans would call on our men to assist them. That way they might be able to shoot at Russians. There was a sortie in the afternoon as well, but His Highness didn't go.

1st August (Saturday)
Unbroken rain all day. No sorties, everything's quiet.

2nd August (Sunday)
It's still raining, the mud is terrible. Nobody wants to set foot outside, everyone stays indoors playing cards, dice, etc.

3rd August (Monday)
The weather's improved. Early in the morning a Stuka gave a demonstration of bombing. It was a pleasure to watch, but it wouldn't have been so good if it had been for real. Managed to do some washing today. We drove down to the Oskol. The water and everything was fine. We had a very good wash ourselves. However, on the way back we got stuck in the terrible mud. We pushed and pulled, but by the time we extricated the car from the

mud around 2 p.m., I was covered in mud from head to foot. We arrived for lunch with me in this state, General [*József*] Németh had been invited to lunch—luckily others took over the serving duties. No flying, though the Russians fly over us every day. They must know by now that we're here. One of these days they'll throw something at us.

4th August (Tuesday)
The airfield's still quite muddy in places, so flying is limited. Guests had been invited for supper: Nándor Zichy, Captain Mocsáry, and Captain Hess, so I had to provide food for them to eat. I got hold of cigarettes, bread, matches, soap etc to barter, and four of us set off. The Russian peasant wouldn't give us anything easily: whatever we wanted, he said it wasn't his, but as soon as we caught a goose or a hen, it was his straight away. He shouted and wailed like mad, but we didn't understand a word of it. The whole village was out on the street. Night was approaching, so we had our guns ready, but we still had a lot to do. We had 2 hens and a chicken, but that was nothing. That cost us 2 loaves of bread. They were afraid of each other, they didn't dare barter with us, though we were offering them sugar or cigarettes. After some effort we managed to get hold of another terribly thin goose, it weighed no more than 1 kg. We set off back, as we had 7 or 8 km to cover. On the way back we picked some cucumbers and onions from vegetable gardens. We got to the Oskol, which is quite deep in places, but not very wide anywhere—about 6 or 7 metres. There's no bridge anywhere. We stripped off and carried our booty across the river, in places the water wasn't even waist deep. On the other side there was a small flock of sheep, but no shepherd. We looked for one without success. He was lying by the ditch watching us, scared of us. We went up to him in a friendly manner and gave him a

big box of cigarettes, 1 kg of sugar and 20 marks. He asked us to take the sheep without anyone seeing. One of the boys chose a nice ram born this year, a nice fat lamb. We stuffed it into a rucksack so the Russians wouldn't see it, at least while we went through the village. My friend nearly ruptured himself, and it was terribly hot as well. The sheep kept quiet, just urinated all down my friend's back, right into his boots. As soon as we got out of the village, we tried to drive it along, but it just wanted to go back. So we tied its legs together, hung it from one of the guns, and carried it on our shoulders all the way back. We worked up a real sweat. At last we got back. We killed the lamb, its meat was nice and gave us a very good supper. There was plenty for anyone who cared to come, because we had to finish it all. We had to pack up, because at 2 a.m. the first section were setting off for Nikolayevka, 186 km further forward, and we were to follow at 7:45. The supper went ahead: there was lamb stew with potatoes, cheese, spring onions, stewed fruit, coffee, biscuits, and excellent drinks.

5th August (Wednesday)

At 2 a.m. general noise and preparations. The first group set off at 2:45 a.m.. Any more sleep was out of the question. Reveille at 4 a.m., and at 5 the planes left too. We left this nice place which we'd got so used to, and it was just as well, because as we got down to the road, it must have been 8 a.m., 3 bombs hit the site of our camp about 500 m away. The Russians have only just started bombing, though they knew we were there. Since then they've visited the airfield frequently; the bombers are still there. The journey was quite good, just long. I won't even mention the animal carcasses along the way. Lots of ammunition with guns on the roadside. As we advance, we can see from one village to the next that the people here are better off. They look better. There are loads of children, 5–10 in each house. Crowds of children, a dozen in front of each house. A Russian tractor towing 2 trailers rolled onto a mine on a bridge. You can see what happened to it, and the bridge, on the picture. [*The picture has not survived.*] One of our trucks, the Botond, was full to bursting with boards for a whole house. It had to work hard, and lumbered along slowly. Got to the new airfield at 7:30 p.m., because we got lost on the way. The children had turned the signposts around. I even had an argument with 2nd Lieutenant Ortutay: he wanted to go left, the way the signpost indicated, while I wanted to go right, following the map. As we were standing there, a car came up, driven by a Hungarian officer. He directed us onto the road indicated by the map, because if we'd gone the way the signpost pointed, we'd have got to the front line in 3 or 4 km. We turned the signposts back so they pointed the right way, and then went on. The nearest town is Nikolayevka, about 5 km away. Naturally there was nowhere to stay. His Highness was accommodated temporarily in one of the tents, while I lay down under an apple tree next to the tent—the whole camp is in a big orchard. Loads of fruit trees, but untended. There's plenty of fruit, and the boys pick it, unripe as it is, and make stewed fruit to go with the honey we get for breakfast. It's very good. The airfield is further from the camp, about 3 km away: they drive there.

6th August (Thursday)

Had to get up at 2:30 a.m., because His Highness was going on a sortie. There's more chance of encountering the enemy here, because today 2 of them have already had to face 36 enemy aircraft. They were greatly outnumbered, and his escort—[*Sergeant Zoltán Nemeslaki*] —had fallen behind, so he was alone. The Ratas pounced on him, but he shot at them and made off. He would certainly have been shot down if he hadn't escaped by going into a dive. He pulled the plane out of the dive close to the ground, and set off back to the camp. By 5 a.m. he'd got back safely. The plane had been hit twice. Nemeslaki landed safely too. He saw one of the attacking aircraft catching fire. Later they found the wreckage of the Rata which had been shot down. The outcome could have been different. They put up the large tent. I put up my tent as well, close by, [*opposite the large one and 5 or 6 m away, so I would always be visible and also able to see everything, and*] to have somewhere to put things and to sleep. When he reported the incident, 8 planes took off but couldn't find any enemy planes, though in the night they'd bombed Korotoyak heavily. His Highness's first kill.

7th August (Friday)

At 4 a.m. the Hawks rumble into life and set off far away to disrupt the Russians' great pleasure in their bombing raids. [*Flight Lt. Horthy took off as well.*] His engine seized up, and he got back at 9 a.m. on a motorcycle. The second group left towards 11, [*Flight Lt. Horthy went with this group too*]. They came back at 1 p.m. very pleased with themselves and congratulating Sergeant Szentgyörgyi on having shot down a Russian plane. However, their celebrations were premature, because the plane which had been shot down landed right here on our airfield, and another one 40 km away. There were 3 wounded Germans in it. So the planes had been German, not Russian. Luckily they didn't know it was our men who had shot them down. They slept here and we gave them food and drink. However, they did find out eventually. [*Squadron Leader Kálmán Csukás of the general staff shot down by mistake a German He-111 reconnaissance plane in the area of Korotoyak.*] The third group got back at 3 p.m.. They suffered a serious loss: Sergeant Péterffy, who had been selected for promotion, was shot down and crashed in flames. There's no way back to life from that. At least we can bury his remains, because he fell on our side of the firing line. The Russians are attacking strongly, in places they've even crossed the Don. We're very close to the front too, 50–60 km away; but we're not expecting to withdraw, because we could only do so with heavy losses. The ammunition store is here too. The good thing is that the Russians aren't bothering us here yet.

8th August (Saturday)
The Russians are throwing everything they've got into a strong land attack with vastly superior numbers: they have 3 or 4 times more men than us. The land forces stand their ground well, and repulse all local breakthroughs during the day. Our bombers help them, but the Russians are bombing heavily as well. The fighters take off too, towards noon. They return with two kills, though they only have 4 working planes, the rest all need minor or major repairs. [*So Flight Lt. Horthy's plane, being one of the four, takes off daily.*] A new group arrived from home today. In the afternoon a good bath in an oil drum which has been cut in half: a stylish bathtub here. During the night the Russians did manage to cross the Don with significant forces, mainly tanks. They broke through by the 6th division [*in fact the 7th light division*], which was the weakest point. We must have suffered heavy losses, as ambulance cars pass continuously, day and night. Major General Szabó will take over command of this division, [*leaving the Vice-Regent, whose military and political adviser he's been until now*].

9th August (Sunday)
General Szabó left to take up his new duties. [*Major General László Szabó took over command of the 6th light*

division on 9th August 1942.] We moved into the new house which he'd occupied up to now, [*a comfortable wooden hut, much better than the tent.*] Did a lot of washing today, as the weather is good, and here there's no such thing as Sundays or feast days. Much aerial activity. Pilot Officer Takács made an emergency landing, we thought he'd disappeared. His Highness went with the second group. Nemeslaki, his escort, fell behind again and disappeared. The Russians are bombing heavily and attacking strongly everywhere. At night they set every village and town alight. We can't put the fires out, and there's nobody to put them out for anyway. Today they went out to bring back the burnt remains of Sergeant Péterffy, who was shot down: we'll bury them here in Nikolayevka. The poor lad was only just 25: he couldn't have imagined that this was where and how he would end his life.

10th August (Monday)

Sortie at 3 a.m., His Highness goes too. The Russians are weakening now, because our men are pushing them hard on land and in the air, together with a few German planes. Pilot Officer Szabó didn't return from the sortie, but it turned out that he'd got lost in the clouds and landed on the previous airfield, where he refuelled and then came back safe and sound. We got news of Nemeslaki too: he'd also got lost and landed at the previous airfield with minor faults, which are being repaired, then he'll bring the plane back. Everyone can see now that the Hawks are barely able to meet the demands placed on them: the Russian planes are much better. It was only commitment and good tactics that made it possible to report by midnight that the Russians had been pushed back across the Don everywhere: though we did suffer losses of both men and materials.

11th August (Tuesday)

His Highness goes in the second sortie at 7 a.m.. In the first we lost Sergeant Gémes, one of our best non-commissioned pilots. He was shot down by the Russian anti-aircraft artillery over enemy territory. We found out later what had happened to him. Those who were with him saw the plane going down in flames, but Gémes ejected, his parachute opened properly, and he came down on the Russian side. They'll probably capture him, and then he won't have an easy time. At midday the deputies Béla Polgár and István Gajzagó came to visit. [*They were parliamentary deputies of the ruling Hungarian Life Party.*] They looked funny side by side in their uniforms. [*Béla Polgár was an enormous sportsman, 2 m tall; Gajzagó was only 165 cm and slim.*] We invited them to lunch. They couldn't stop praising the food, which I can understand as we certainly do have good food and plenty of it. At 5:30 p.m. a football match between the Szolnok and Kolozsvár [*Cluj-Napoca, Romania*] companies. His Highness played too. Lots of laughter, etc. A German pilot officer was here for supper, he'd been shot down by the Russians too, but he'd managed to get back across. Nemeslaki got back too after a long journey. Pilot Officer Takács is going home on the hospital train. He's wounded in two places: his arm and his thigh.

12th August (Wednesday)

His Highness feels unwell and spends the whole day reading. The weather is good; he sits in his folding chair. It seems to be some kind of stomach upset with diarrhoea, but might also be an infection. We make a garden to occupy ourselves. There's a building belonging to the collective farm near us in the orchard. There's a T-34 here which has been shot down, but it's not burnt out.

13th August (Thursday)
His Highness is still unwell, stomach-ache and colic. He hardly sets foot outside. He reads a bit, but feels ill. He doesn't consult a doctor, even though there is one here, Captain Rátvai. He takes one or two carbon tablets and doesn't eat anything. Some improvement by evening.

14th August (Friday)
He feels better, but still isn't fully fit. Get a message that Her Highness will arrive in Kiev today on the Red Cross train. Pack quickly. Leave pass; military passport. A Storch plane is made available; we leave. Arrive at Konotop airfield at 12:30 p.m.; refuel, and rest a little. Get to Kiev by 5:30 p.m.; it's raining. Wait half an hour, then we're driven into the town. We are accommodated in a large villa, which apparently used to belong to the former party secretary of the Ukraine. Now it's occupied by a high-ranking German officer, but he's moved out for us this weekend. The rooms are nicely furnished, but the black marble bathroom with white bath and washbasin is peculiar. Hot water! Just the two of us in the house today; Her Highness will arrive on the train tomorrow. There's a woman of around 30 here, she hands the place over to me. I don't know who she is and what her job is; I don't ask whether she's Russian or German—she speaks both languages. I know enough German to ask questions and understand the answers. I'm sure she's not Russian. She moves freely around the room, arranging vases. Supper in a restaurant. [*Conditions like at home; plenty of everything.*] There's no war here. Bath and rest.

15th August (Saturday)
His Highness is taken on a tour of the town. Lunch in his honour. We're very well looked after. The train will arrive at 9:30 tonight. A big bunch of flowers is brought to welcome Her Highness. War correspondents film and

take photos. Supper. I look over and arrange everything in the house. The cleaning staff have cleaned it well during the day.

Staff Sergeant Viktor Tornyi of the Guards came on the train too. He brought a letter and a parcel for me. We talked for a long time. He's staying somewhere near here. Though it was quite late and Her Highness had just arrived after a tiring journey, Their Highnesses talked for a long time in the lounge.

16th August (Sunday)

Get up late. A large breakfast is brought, which I serve. At 11 a.m. they go to visit a hospital. They talk to the patients. The doctors tell them about the hospital and how the patients are looked after. I can tell from the conversations that Her Highness is very well informed, she mentions several patients by name. Lunch in the restaurant. In the afternoon the two of them walk along the bank of the Dnieper and in the town. [*I follow at a discreet distance.*] Had the afternoon off: went out to the stadium and watched a football match between Hungarian and German teams—the result was 4:0. [*Supper in the restaurant, and we're back at the house by 10 p.m..*]

17th August (Monday)

They're due at the hospital at 11:00; until then they can rest. Slept till 9:00, then went to wake them, but they were already awake. Rest and sleep in the afternoon. [*There's nobody in the house apart from us. A quick supper in the restaurant, then back home.*]

18th August (Tuesday)

Pack again, a quick lunch, then set off back. Said our goodbyes, and Her Highness came out to the airport with us. [*We were driven there in a large Adler car.*] Said goodbye to Her Highness, and at 2 p.m. we were airborne and on our way back. Got to our airfield in Nikolayevka at 5:30 p.m.. They're playing football here too. There are Germans in the tent next to ours: 5 or 6 of them, they came here a few days ago. What are these doing here, I ask Sándor Horváth, who's sharing my tent. They've been here one or two days. [*They're signalmen, he says. Staff Sergeant Harmath of the Guards doesn't know any more either, just that they're Germans and they've just arrived. General Szabó isn't here any more, and 2nd Lieutenant Ortutay doesn't know anything about them either.*]

19th August (Wednesday)

His Highness tells me that tomorrow he will start a tour of inspection of the Hungarian forces. We'll leave at 10 a.m. in the plane we had yesterday, and first of all we'll visit the Szombathely armoured division which is now under the command of General Szabó. [*Major General László Szabó had been appointed commander of the 6th light division—see earlier.*] Then at the beginning of September we're going home. We've been left very much on our own. [*In the afternoon His Highness went out to see his plane, which had been undergoing minor repairs while we were away. He found it in good order.*] Towards evening he asks for a bottle of brandy and takes it with him when he goes to play cards with Squadron Leader Csukás. He comes back around 10 p.m. and tells me to wake him at 4:30 a.m., because he's going on one last sortie. He brought the brandy back unopened because nobody had wanted any. He asked the sentry to wake me at 4:00.

20th August 1942 (Thursday)

Woken at 4:00; get dressed quickly. Bring a thermos of coffee from the cooks. Wake His Highness at 4:30; he gets dressed quickly. The car turns up. Nemeslaki is here, and somebody else; he offers them coffee, but they don't want any.

He tells me that the plan for today hasn't changed. I understand; there's still plenty of time to pack. The planes drone off and circle over the camp as usual. [*He waved from the plane.*] The sun's already up. I'm sitting on the bench under the pear tree, when 2nd Lieutenant Fehér comes running up, looking for me. He can hardly speak, but tells me that the Vice-Regent's plane has crashed and he's dead. [*The bombers have just telephoned; the ambulance people are already by the plane and are burying it so it doesn't burn out.*] Run to the squadron leader, who's standing outside his tent in his boots, his coat over his pyjamas, his hat on his head. "István, start the car so it warms up," I say to the driver. Quickly we get into the Horch jeep and drive straight to the scene through a field of sunflowers. We find the plane already buried. Nobody's allowed near it because there's a danger it might explode. I have my camera with me and take photos undisturbed. Later we return to the scene, by then many high-ranking German and Hungarian officers are there. I easily recognise the body. I identify the objects and verify that they belong to him. A coffin is made from the door of the hospital in Nikolayevka.

21st August (Friday)

Leave for home on road no. 21, in ambulance car no. 21, on the 21st of the month. I don't see the Germans around, but I'm not interested in them any more.

György Német:
AN ORPHANED CAMP

Eastern front, August

We are in the Szolnok fighter pilots' camp.

We walk around under the fruit trees, deeply moved.

This was where Vitéz István [*Hungarian for Stephen*] Horthy had worked, rested, and made plans... [*the Vitézi Rend, or Order of the Brave, was created by the Regent Miklós Horthy and conferred on those who had fought with gallantry in the first world war. Those who received the honour were also entitled to grants of land; the honour was hereditary and passed to the eldest son*].

His area was a quiet, shady part of the orchard. This was where the Vice-Regent had stayed.

A decorative wood memorial stands outside the simple wooden hut. Artistically carved, and decorated with the mythical bird of the ancient Magyars, it was presented by the flying train technical company and placed here a week ago. Around the base are small Soviet mines; on the planed surfaces are tasteful poker-work flying scenes. In front of it the Hungarian coat of arms with the double cross has been laid out in coloured pebbles. The men vied with each other to clean and tidy up the whole area under the fruit trees with loving care, though nobody had asked or ordered them to do so. Willow branches bent into semicircles line the small winding paths around the quarters.

Moved, I step over the threshold into vitéz István Horthy's room.

The small wooden hut is a single room 2 metres square.

In the middle is the door, and on either side there are small windows. To the left of the entrance is a simple camp bed. A table, a chair, a washbasin.

Suitcases.

György—Gyuri—Farkas, his favourite valet, tidies up the room silently.

The valet had knocked nails into the wooden wall to serve as clothes hooks.

He had made a mosquito net holder out of willow branches to go over the colourful bed.

I glance around at the belongings which no longer have an owner.

Each little thing is a precious memory.

Here is his camera, and his grey and burgundy striped pyjamas.

A pair of boots, a pair of officer's shoes, a yellow woollen blanket.

A shiny pilot's helmet almost smiles on the suitcase. Next to it a pair of thick leather gloves, creased and battered, speak of heights and distances which he longed for and which he conquered so many times...

In the right-hand corner of the room, under large maps, is a wash stand built out of thick branches. On it is a simple washbasin. His own machine-gun hangs on a nail in the corner.

On a small chair next to the bed is a radio set. He got it from Major General Vitéz László Szabó, and heard the Regent's radio message on it a few days ago.

There is some exercise equipment here: he liked to keep fit, and whenever he could, he set aside a few minutes each day for doing exercises.

On the table, packed in cellophane, are the biscuits which every pilot gets. He hadn't taken them with him. There's a small pile of loose change on the table: one pengő sixty fillérs, and a few pfennigs.

And here's the folding chair.

"He really liked this chair," says the valet, "it's a folding hunter's chair. The Regent sent it to him. He used to sit in it under the pear tree, reading or thinking…"

Gyuri the valet carries on tidying and packing. He is a fresh-faced young Hungarian lad, black haired. His father was a tradesman, disabled in the first world war. His widowed mother lives in Dabod, in the Bácska region of southern Hungary. Vitéz István Horthy took Gyuri Farkas on years ago, before he was married. The Hungarian orphan lad was a faithful and reliable servant.

"It'll make a difference to a lot of people, me included…" says Gyuri. "When I was with him, I felt like his brother. Here at the airfield as well everyone liked him as if he were a close relative or friend…

"His Highness always left everything to me. If we were going somewhere, he just told me how long he would be away and he knew I'd take care of everything. Often, in fact nearly always, I went with him, we mostly travelled together. I went with him on his last trip too: he went to Kiev to see Her Highness. We got back on Tuesday evening at half past five in an Aradó plane which he piloted.

"When he came back from a sortie he always came in here first, washed, and had breakfast. And over breakfast he'd tell me all about it. As if it was my brother talking.

"Last night we went to bed at half past ten. He had supper outside with the officers, they had lentil soup with tinned meat. Afterwards some German officers came and he talked with them. Then I came in here with him so I'd be here if he needed anything.

"This morning at a quarter past four I knocked on the door, which he'd bolted from the inside so the wind wouldn't blow it open. He woke up at once, opened the door, and asked what time it was. "Won't we be late?" he asked then. I told him that the others going on the sortie with him were just getting up. Sergeant Zoltán Nemeslaki was piloting the other Hawk; I told him that the sergeant was just getting dressed. He got dressed in a few minutes, he put on his standard issue uniform. He took one Aktedron [*medicine*] tablet with a mouthful of water and ran to his plane. All pilots get this Aktedron. He didn't eat anything else. Before leaving he told me to sort out his dress uniform because at 10 o'clock he had to go in a Storch plane to inspect one of the divisions. "Make sure the boots are gleaming," he said, as I remember. He always liked it if everything he was wearing was clean...

"I ran after him to the plane with some coffee, because the cooks were a bit late with breakfast for those going on the sortie. I said: "I've brought some hot coffee." He didn't take it, because the others hadn't got any.

"Then they left, and I came back here and got his things ready. At half past five 2nd Lieutenant Fehér came running up breathlessly, and told me that the Vice-Regent had crashed."

Gyuri Farkas falls silent. He looks down at the pair of boots he is holding in his hands.

"He wore these boots for the first time yesterday."

I look once more around the quiet little room, then go out to the big table under the sighing pear tree, where Vitéz István Horthy used to eat with his fellow officers.

(This report by the journalist György Német, an officer designate serving his year in the ranks as a war correspondent, appeared in "Új Magyarország" [*New Hungary*] on 28th August.)

György Farkas:
FIFTY YEARS ON

As I turn the pages of the diary I wrote in the summer of 1942, the short notes written on the squared paper of my exercise book help me to recall the events of fifty years ago. I can still see clearly everything that happened. People, objects, and dates appear and link up with each other in a chain. A diary means most to the person who wrote it, because everything that happened is still vividly present in that person's mind; however, people reading it later can also find in it explanations for various details. But even for the diarist several connections become clear only later: connections which at the time, when he was young and in the turmoil of events, he didn't see or couldn't understand.

István Horthy, who since 19th February 1942 had been the country's Vice-Regent, joined the 1st Fighter Division in Szolnok for military service on 1st May 1942. As his valet, I joined up too. We stayed in the county hall as guests of the Lord Lieutenant, but had our meals at the airfield. On Saturdays we went home to Budapest, returning to Szolnok on Mondays.

A month later—as can be seen in my diary—on 5th June, I set off for the front with the ground crews. I took with me everything which my master and I might need during our time in the camp. I had a separate inventory of all the bags, objects and equipment, so that I would be able to find everything quickly when it was needed.

My master only arrived at the theatre of war a month later, on 2nd July, with the pilots. I could hardly wait for him to come and was very pleased when he finally arrived. At the time it never occurred to me to wonder what the second most important person in the country was doing out at the front, his life exposed to constant danger. Just another reserve flying officer among many thousands who obey orders, carry out instructions, and stand firm together with the men where necessary. They fight, they fly sorties, they risk their lives. Pilots were almost constantly dicing with death. And as for those horrible top-heavy Hawks which so easily overturned on landing! How many of them did just that—including one with my master, István Horthy, the Vice-Regent, sitting inside—on the bad and bumpy camp airfields! And the sorties—real combat situations in which you literally have to look death in the face!

This thought still troubles me fifty years on. Why did he have to go out to the front? Why did he have to fight virtually like a private—in the course of not quite two months he flew more than twenty sorties—and why did he have to crash and die in circumstances which remain suspiciously unclarified to this day?

As Vice-Regent, his constitutional status would have allowed him to take a high military rank—that of general—for his tour of inspection of the forces fighting on the eastern front.

Of course I can understand him: I know how modest he was and how he wouldn't tolerate preferential treatment, how much he liked his fellow pilots and how he had dedicated his life to flying. He wanted to be with them in danger as well. But the decision—which was certainly not his—was still wrong. How could they allow István Horthy, the man in whose hands they wanted to place the country in those difficult times, to go to such a place?

I can well understand how Squadron Leader Kálmán Csukás, the commander of the flying division, felt. He practically broke down when he received the terrible news at dawn on 20th August, there in front of his tent, half dressed. Perhaps this outstanding pilot and humane commander whom everybody respected and liked, who kept one-time sporting friends together at the front in a close-knit community of colleagues, felt that he too was responsible for what had happened. After all it was he who had given the order for the sortie the previous evening. If only he had known that General Gusztáv Jány, commander of the Hungarian 2nd Army, had told the Vice-Regent the same day that he had completed his flying service at the front! (Perhaps fate had a hand in the fact that Kálmán Csukás also died a heroic death on the eastern front that same autumn.)

He and I went out together to the scene of the accident, to the crashed plane containing the country's Vice-Regent—or rather what remained of him. The plane was still smoking. The smoke, like that of Cain's sacrifice, wriggled along the ground like a long, treacherous snake. We looked helplessly at the scene, thoughts racing through our minds. It can't be true! We looked, not comprehending what had happened. Had it crashed? But how? The plane—the heap of wreckage—was lying belly down, its undercarriage raised and locked. The heated and deformed mass of metal had not yet cooled down. They buried it, not to be opened up until the afternoon. Until then it ought to be guarded. But by whom? And from whom? Officials and onlookers came and went, Hungarians and Germans. In the afternoon: opening up, examination, identification, official record. Everyone saw something different, everyone saw it differently and gave a different account. For instance corporal Rafael Mészáros from the Huszt [*Khust, Ukraine*] battalion saw that the plane was on fire as it fell—but he wasn't even questioned. Only the findings of the medical record leave no room for doubt: there before the doctor is the body, the shattered and burnt remains of a man who not long ago was still alive; and all that can be found goes into the doctor's dreadful inventory. This is the truth: the rest is just imagination, details seen and half seen in fractions of a moment.

But what could have caused the accident? What made the plane crash? Nobody examined the wreckage for clues. The remains of the plane were dispersed; they were not kept for a technical committee to examine later in detail, component by component, in order to try and determine the cause.

We found out later that István Horthy had fired his flares before the crash. What was he trying to indicate? That his plane had gone out of control? Or was he trying to signal to the reconnaissance plane that he was unable to follow? Who can tell?

We walked around the wreckage. I looked over the immediate surroundings as well. I found a piece of my master's skull on the ground 15–20 metres from the plane. It was covered with skin and hair. I had my camera with me and took photographs of the buried wreckage. Then early in the afternoon we went back and opened it up. I was one of those who helped to lift the body out. It was an awful sight. When we removed the plane's armour, a fairly heavy half oval shaped plate 100×120 cm in size and about 20 mm thick, we found the body: sitting, the right side of his forehead smashed by the right-hand machine gun. This must be where the piece of skull I found lying on the ground came from. The stump of his right hand was on the joystick, the left near the canopy exit button. His legs were drawn up in a seated position. His arms and legs were burnt. His wristwatch had stopped at 5:07. His clothes were burnt off on both sides, all that was left was what had been covered by the armour and the earth. All that was in his pocket was his pocket knife. He wasn't wearing a dog-tag, so I identified him for the official record on the basis of the objects and what I could recognise.

Meanwhile a coffin was prepared and brought from the hospital in Nikolayevka. We put the body, doubled up as it was, into a tin coffin and placed that in the wooden coffin. We laid out the body in the camp, and the officers and men formed a guard of honour. There were plenty of wreaths and flowers. Everyone was moved; everyone was silent.

The following day, the 21st, we took the coffin in an ambulance to Stary Oskol, where after a brief funeral service we boarded a train and left for home. The papers of the time published detailed accounts of each stage of the funeral procession. The official funeral was held on 27th August at 10 a.m. in the domed hall of the Parliament building. My wife and I were among those invited to attend. The burial took place later the same day, a Thursday, at Kenderes, where my master, István Horthy, Vice-Regent of Hungary, was laid to rest in the family mausoleum, in which he remains to this day.

Of course, after the burial people started to speculate as to what had happened, what could have caused the tragedy—which is only natural. But there were stupid gossips and ill-intentioned slanderers who had "certain" knowledge of some drunken revelry celebrating my master's name-day (the feast of St István [*Saint Stephen*]). These people had no idea of the kind of person István Horthy was, or of the conditions he was living in at the front. If anyone knows, then I know what he drank and how much, because during the last five years of his life I was almost constantly at his side, and I served him. If he returned from somewhere, I would talk to him within a couple of hours, and would have noticed if he was drunk. István Horthy and the rest of the Horthy family were extremely abstemious. A cup of tea in the morning, a glass of soda water at lunch-time, sometimes a glass of beer in the evening; in the summer heat occasionally a glass of whisky, after polo matches a large glass of soda water, in company at dinner a glass or two of wine: this is what my master's "heavy drinking" amounted to.

There were also rumours of a deliberate attempt on his life, saying that the Germans had had a hand in the affair. It was well known that Hitler disliked István Horthy because he was pro-British. When he was elected Vice-Regent, Hitler didn't even send a telegram of congratulation. It's also true that the Germans were constantly there with us in the area, on the airfield, and everywhere. There had even been an incident when German planes fired at István Horthy's plane "by mistake." And they could also gain access to the Hungarian planes on our airfield. Nobody can prove anything now, but the suspicion cannot be dispelled.

A few days after the burial the Regent summoned me to his office. To my surprise, the prime minister, Mr Miklós Kállay, and the defence minister, Mr Károly Bartha, were there too. They wanted to know my opinion. The Regent knew me well, I met him and was able to talk to him every day, since as a bachelor I'd been the only member of the staff who could live in the Regent's apartment. Most of the times we met, he would stop me and say a few words beyond simply acknowledging my greeting. In any case, he knew all his employees by name, not only in the Castle but also at Gödöllő and Kenderes. So I felt free to tell him what I thought about his son's death. Of course I didn't say how much Hitler infuriated him: the Regent clearly knew that without me having to tell him. But I gave a detailed account of the last days, and the visit to Kiev. I went so far as to comment that even if he'd been at the front simply as a flying officer, I wouldn't have let him go into action so many times; and if he was there as Vice-Regent, he shouldn't have been allowed to risk his life like an ordinary soldier.

That was the gist of what I had to say, even if I didn't say it in so many words at the time; and my opinion is still the same now.

The Regent ordered the most rigorous investigation, but whatever the investigation could subsequently uncover, it couldn't bring István Horthy back to life.

WITNESSES RECALL THE EVENTS OF 50 YEARS AGO

FORMER ACTING PILOT OFFICER KÁROLY WÁGNER

Károly Wágner started his pilot's training in Pécs in 1938. In 1940 he became an acting pilot officer. In 1941 he started his service in the tactical reconnaissance squadron at Kaposvár-Taszár. He took part in the incursion into northern Yugoslavia in April 1941, flying over enemy territory on four occasions. After that he served on the eastern front. His reconnaissance plane was shot down on 5th July 1941 beyond the north eastern Carpathians, over Dolina in the Ukraine. He was hidden by a Ukrainian peasant for six days, until the Hungarian forces arrived.

From June to October 1942 he served with the 3/2 tactical reconnaissance squadron. In his Heinkel He-46 reconnaissance plane he flew 41 missions over enemy territory, mainly in the battles along the Don.

In the early morning of 20th August 1942 it was Acting Pilot Officer Wágner who was piloting the reconnaissance plane which was to be escorted by István Horthy and Zoltán Nemeslaki in their fighters. In a letter written to István Horthy's widow he looks back on the events, giving an account of what happened 50 years ago and amplifying the brief official record made at the time.

"On Thursday 20th August 1942 at 5 am, as a squad leader in the 3/2 tactical reconnaissance squadron (at the time my rank was acting pilot officer), I was sitting in the pilot's seat of the He-46 reconnaissance plane, which was warmed up and ready to go. Behind me was the observer, Elek Baranyi, a captain in the infantry and commander of the plane. We were waiting for the fighters. A messenger ran up to the plane and shouted: 'The fighters have been delayed!' A little later 2 pairs of fighters appeared above us. The first reconnaissance plane started up immediately, and soon disappeared from view, accompanied by two fighters. By this time I was airborne too, and swung round to the left towards the usual hillside in order to try out our machine guns. It was late summer, and the morning sun cast long shadows over the forested and undulating area.

I dived, and both my observer and I fired at the hillside; then I pulled the plane into a steep climb, and looked behind me to the left for the fighters. While still climbing steeply, I caught sight of two fighters slightly below and about 300 metres behind me. In the same moment the leading plane of the pair banked to the left and went into an increasingly sharp, over-banked turn, then its nose dropped and it fell into a near-vertical spin.

Shocked, I watched it and started counting the turns, which I could see very clearly. One, two—at this point I sensed that he wouldn't be able to pull that heavy plane out of the dive. Three, four, five. A little after the fifth turn it hit the ground. Immediately a flame several metres high exploded upwards and a thick black column of smoke was formed; it rose in the gentle breeze, clearly visible against the background of the forest, which was still in shadow.

The crash happened incredibly fast. It took 6–8 seconds—I can only express the time in seconds, because the plane was moving fast and low down.

'Take photos, sir, take photos!' I shouted to my observer; at the same time I made a sharp left turn and pushed my plane down to 15–20 metres above the ground, and circled two or three times over the burning and smoking plane. I was in a state of shock and great consternation. My first thought was to try and land by the plane: perhaps we would be able to help; my second thought was that there was nothing we could do, he couldn't have survived that crash.

I lost sight of the second fighter of the pair; it had been wobbling strangely while the first was corkscrewing down.

Then I pulled up again and landed with a full complement of bombs at my airfield, 1–1.5 km away as the crow flies. The tail-skid broke off.

In my opinion the most significant part of this tragic event was something which no other air crews and nobody else apart from us mentioned when they were questioned, but which I saw perfectly clearly: Flight Lt. István Horthy fired his flares before crashing.

The fact that the flares exploded into reddish stars by the second turn proves that they had been fired by the pilot, using the flare gun which was in its holder ready to fire. These small luminous bodies, 4 or 5 of them, then fell—from my angle—parallel to the falling plane, as if escorting it.

You do not need to know too much about ballistics to understand that when fired, a flare only explodes once it is at a safe distance of 40–50 metres from the plane, discharging an appropriate number of burning luminous bodies.

However, this proves that Flight Lt. Horthy had fired his flares deliberately immediately before his plane went into the dive, when it was still in a horizontal position. He had to make the decision, reach over (the flare gun was in an open tube at the side), and pull the trigger to fire the gun. This raises a number of questions:

1. What was he trying to indicate to us and to the other fighter pilot?
2. What happened in the plane and to the plane during the flight and before it crashed?

3. Why did those responsible at the time fail to consider Flight Lt. Horthy's last act of firing the flares? This despite the fact that Captain Elek Baranyi stated that he did so, and Acting Pilot Officer Károly Wágner's statement agreed with Captain Baranyi's, as can be seen in the official record, which is in the Hungarian Military History Archive. [*see Documents*]

The wreckage of the Hawk plane was removed and taken away the next day (Friday), after the usual accident inspection and after the chief mechanic and the maintenance personnel had been questioned for the official record. However, two questions remain unanswered:

1. What caused the crash?
2. Why did Flight Lt. István Horthy, Vice-Regent of Hungary, act as he did in the last minutes of his life?

My own plane, a He-46, had the same flare firing equipment, which was within easy reach of the pilot's seat. Its function was to signal to our own anti-aircraft defences if they should fire at us that we were not the enemy. The number of luminous bodies discharged was changed every day at noon and kept confidential between ourselves and the Hungarian anti-aircraft defence formations.

This does not prove that the pilot was lacking in skill. The plane banked sharply, stalled, and then suddenly dropped its nose and fell into a spin as a result of a mechanical fault which was presumably already present and which the pilot, Flight Lt. Horthy, attempted to signal to us by means of the flare he fired himself just before.

This is the decisive fact! The plane must have gone into this low-speed over-banked turn and stalled of its own accord, despite the actions of Flight Lt. Horthy, and in this awful predicament—in the last phase—all he could do was fire his flare to let us know that he was in deep trouble.

This fatal situation is also confirmed by the statement of Acting Pilot Officer Gyula Szabó, who as the reconnaissance squadron's duty officer that day watched the plane's flight from the ground. He states: '...the other [*plane*] was to the right of it, and flying roughly along the river, it made an over-banked and increasingly tight sideslipping turn and headed towards the forest north of the airfield. As the plane got near the forest, still in a banked position, its nose dropped.' So this was a fairly long period of flight. My own observation joins on to this one, as if continuing on from it.

These two observations were made completely independently of each other—one from the ground, the other from the air. Both suggest that the plane was out of control.

Acting Pilot Officer Gyula Szabó's statement can also be found in the Military History Archive. [*See Documents*] I knew nothing about the questioning and statement of Acting Pilot Officer Gyula Szabó until 30th July 1990, when friends in Hungary presented me with a book published in Budapest and entitled '1942. aug. 20. 5 óra 7 perc - Horthy István repülő főhadnagy és kora eltérő megközelítésben' [*20th August 1942, 0507 Hours—Flight Lt. István Horthy and His Time: A Different Approach*]."

That concludes the account of former Acting Pilot Officer Károly Wágner.

AN UNUSUAL WITNESS: FORMER CORPORAL RAFAEL MÉSZÁROS

Reserve Corporal Rafael Mészáros served at the front with the 54/II. Huszt battalion. He was a motorcycle messenger and observer. His duties required him to be reliable and to have good powers of observation. Corporal Mészáros came from western Hungary, and his battalion was stationed right next to the 1st fighter division's airfield.

Rafael Mészáros is now 77, but his agility and lively mind belie his age. His memory of distant events is remarkable: he knows place names by heart, he describes what was happening around him, where, and when, who his commanding officers were, who gave him what orders, and how he carried these out. Although he was not a regular soldier, his behaviour and bearing are military and erect.

He responds to György Farkas' questions with this account of what he saw at dawn on 20th August 1942:

"Well, it was 2 a.m. when I took over observation duty. My binoculars were around my neck, my pistol in my belt. I had to observe the air-space and listen for any sound. There was deep silence: no gunfire, not even a rifle shot to be heard. No sound from a plane, a tank, or even a car. Gradually it started getting light. It was exactly 5 a.m. when the planes started up on the neighbouring airfield. I watched them taking off through my binoculars. I knew they were Hungarian planes from the direction of the sound, but I also definitely recognised their markings through my binoculars. A Hungarian fighter was coming towards the airfield, flying east to west. I recognised it easily with binoculars and also with the naked eye. It was 3 minutes past 5, I looked at my watch. I couldn't believe my eyes—the plane was on fire! I saw a yellow flame on its side, but no shot anywhere. Why was the side of the plane on fire, where was that flaming yellow trail coming from? Then the dull, distant sound of an impact, and then silence. I immediately reported what I'd seen to Captain Fraknói, my commanding officer. Captain Miklós Fraknói acknowledged my report. Lieutenants Endre Antony and László Palotai were present too. I knew our district and the terrain around us well, the whole area, as I'd been around it several times. Lieutenant Antony instructed me to take him quickly by motorcycle to where the plane might have crashed. It was nearby, we arrived quickly at the scene. Soldiers were already there who must have been even closer to the scene, they were already burying the plane so it wouldn't burn out. That was when I found out that it was the Vice-Regent's plane. I had thought he would make it to the airfield in the burning plane, but there was a low hill there, and the plane crashed nose first into it.

I'm sure the plane wasn't shot down, because I was so close that I would have heard the shot. I saw the yellow flame on the side of the plane with the naked eye too. When they made the TV film, I told Béla Császár, whom I know, that the crash didn't happen the way he showed it, because the plane was coming in smoothly, as if to land, but didn't make it to the airfield."

This is how Reserve Corporal Rafael Mészáros remembers what he saw.

THE OBSERVATIONS OF FORMER STAFF SERGEANT JÓZSEF EGERSZÖGI

József Egerszögi, now in his 78th year, started his military service on 5th October 1936 at the Miskolc airfield. In 1938 he completed an armaments and bomb officer's course in Székesfehérvár, then a one-year non-commissioned officer training course in the same place, and in 1943 he completed a warrant officer training course in Jutas. He served in the air force for 12 years.

József Egerszögi left Kecskemét with the 3/2 tactical reconnaissance squadron in June 1942 for the eastern front. He served on the Ilovskoye-Alekseyevka airfield. He knew Flight Lt. István Horthy personally, and frequently spoke to him. He remembers István Horthy with deep admiration and affection. He saw the crash of the V-421 Hawk from the reconnaissance airfield, which was very close by. This is his account:

"On 20th August 1942 at 5 a.m. two of our He-46 reconnaissance planes left on a mission, each escorted by 2 fighters. The two fighters arrived on time as I was repairing the machine gun on one of the planes. While they were waiting for the reconnaissance plane, the two fighters circled at about 300 metres, then on the second circle the first plane made an over-banked turn and fell, slipping outwards because it had slowed down, then crashed into the undulating ground. I immediately rushed to the scene of the accident, because it had crashed 500–600 metres from us, but unfortunately I couldn't get near it because the machine gun bullets were exploding due to the fire. Sometimes upright, sometimes crawling,

I tried to get there as quickly as possible, I wanted to get to the burning plane, even risking my life to do so, though I knew that nobody in it could have survived. As I threw the first spadeful of earth onto the plane I saw a blackened head which had fallen forward, and an elbow on the left-hand side of the seat. While we were putting out the fire, the rest of the squadron arrived as well. About 15-20 minutes later Squadron Leader Csukás arrived with the other fighter crews, and saluted stiffly before the wreckage. At that time I didn't know who the dead man was. I asked one of the fighter pilots, and he told me in tears that it was the Vice-Regent. Then we left the scene, and the fighter crews took over in order to recover the body and gather up the wreckage. We put up a birch cross—I have kept the photo of it to this day. I know that he was a hero who ended his life prematurely, like so many of his fellow pilots. It moves me to tears to think about them."

DOCUMENTS

Statement by Captain Elek Baranyi for the official record, with a hand-written annotation by Károly Wágner dated 18th September 1991 in Malmö (Military History Archive)

OFFICIAL RECORD

of the interview of Captain Elek Baranyi by the local accident investigation committee, made on 20th August 1942 at 1100 hours in the area of the 3/2 tactical reconnaissance squadron, in the matter of the accident involving His Highness the Vice-Regent Vitéz István Horthy de Nagybánya. Captain Baranyi, as observer, was in command of the aeroplane which His Highness was to protect.

1. Captain, please tell us what you know about how the accident happened.

Item 1. The pair of planes due to escort me arrived at the appointed time at a height of about 350 m over the reconnaissance airfield. where they described a large circle. Meanwhile, having tested the reconnaissance plane's machine guns, I waited for the escorting planes to catch up, and then, heading for Korotoyak at a height of 200 m, I looked back to the right to see if the fighters were following. At that moment the fighters were flying behind me to the right, about 400 m away and about 100 m above me. No sooner had I looked back, about 1 or 2 seconds later, I noticed the leading plane of the pair making a sharp turn downwards to the left, then going into a left-hand spin. The plane made about three turns before hitting the ground. The last turns were flatter, so that I thought it might be possible to prevent the plane crashing. However, the plane could not avoid hitting the ground, and at the moment when it crashed an enormous flame shot out of it—it exploded.

2. Do you have anything more to add?

Item 2. About halfway through the spin I noticed that stars fired from a flare gun were falling near the plane.

When I saw the crashed plane exploding, I circled low over it, and established that the plane and its pilot could not be saved. During this low flight, at the suggestion of my pilot, I took photographs of the burning plane with a hand-held camera. Then I landed and reported the incident by telephone to the duty officer of the fighter division and then to my commanding officer.

3. Is this an accurate record of your statement?

Item 3. Yes.

Date as above. Signatures: Captain Elek Baranyi; members of the investigation committee.

Hand-written annotation by Károly Wágner:

In the He-46 the observer sits with his back to the pilot, so that something which is on the pilot's left will be on the observer's right. Malmö, 18th Szeptember 1991. Wágner.

Statement by Acting Pilot Officer Gyula Szabó for the official record (Military History Archive)

OFFICIAL RECORD
of the interview with Acting Pilot Officer Gyula Szabó, made on 20th August 1942 at 1130 hours in the area of the 3/2 tactical reconnaissance squadron, in the matter of the accident involving His Highness the Vice-Regent Vitéz István Horthy de Nagybánya. Acting Pilot Officer Szabó, as duty officer of the above squadron, witnessed the accident.

1. Acting Pilot Officer, please tell us what you know about how the accident happened.

Item 1. As duty officer, I was standing at the edge of the airfield when our planes left, and as our planes left I saw four fighters in the airspace over our airfield at a height of about 400 m. Two of these planes turned from a northerly direction and headed for Nikolayevka. One of the planes was approaching the airfield in a straight line from the direction of Nikolayevka, while the other was to the right of it, and flying roughly along the river, it made an over-banked and increasingly tight sideslipping turn and headed towards the forest north of the airfield. As the plane got near the forest, still in a banked position, its nose dropped. A few seconds later I heard a powerful explosion from the valley, and immediately afterwards I saw a large column of smoke. I reported this immediately to the duty officer of the fighter division, at about 0515 hours.

2. Do you have anything more to add?

Item 2. I observed nothing else, as I could not see the plane crashing due to the forest between us.

3. Is this an accurate record of your statement?

Item 3. Yes.

Date as above. Signatures: Acting Pilot Officer Gyula Szabó; members of the investigation committee.

Statement by Acting Pilot Officer Károly Wágner for the official record (Military History Archive)

OFFICIAL RECORD

of the interview with Acting Pilot Officer Károly Wágner, made on 20th August 1942 at 1200 hours in the area of the 3/2 tactical reconnaissance squadron, in the matter of the accident involving His Highness the Vice-Regent Vitéz István Horthy de Nagybánya. Acting Pilot Officer Wágner was the pilot of the reconnaissance plane which was to be escorted.

1. Acting Pilot Officer, please tell us what you know about how the accident happened.

Item 1. My observation corresponds completely with the statement made by Captain Baranyi, except that I would like to state that in my view the spin did not flatten out.

2. Do you have anything more to add?

Item 2. I had the impression that the plane fell into a spin having stalled in an over-banked turn made at low speed.

3. Is this an accurate record of your statement?

Item 3. Yes.

Date as above. Signatures: Acting Pilot Officer Károly Wágner; members of the investigation committee.

Statement by Reserve Private György Farkas for the official record (Military History Archive)

OFFICIAL RECORD

of the interview with Reserve Private György Farkas, made at the Ilovskoye military airfield at the command post of the long range reconnaissance division on 20th August 1942 at 2135 hours, in the investigation of the circumstances of the heroic death of His Highness Vitéz István Horthy de Nagybánya, Vice-Regent of Hungary, by the committee appointed by His Majesty's 1st National Defence Flying Group Command, in the presence of the undersigned. The witness gave the following responses to the questions put to him.

1. In what capacity did you serve His Highness the Vice-Regent?

1. I have been His Highness the Vice-Regent's personal valet since 1st September 1937. I accompanied him on active service as a secondary reserve soldier.

2. Were you present in the morning when the Vice-Regent got dressed and left?

2. I woke His Highness the Vice-Regent this morning at 0415 hours and helped him to dress. His Highness put on brown shoes, then a green standard issue camp shirt and his standard issue uniform, and green flying overalls on top. On his tunic His Highness wore two rows of decoration ribbons, with 4 ribbons in each row. In the first row were the miniature star of the Middle Cross of the

Hungarian Order of Merit on a green ribbon, the ribbon of the Knights' Cross with a miniature cross, and the Northern Region and Transylvania memorial medals; in the second row were the Southern Region memorial medal, the miniature star of the Grand Cross of the Italian Order of the Crown on its ribbon, the miniature star of the Grand Cross of the Bulgarian Order of the Crown on its ribbon, and the miniature star of the Middle Cross of the Finnish Order of the White Rose on its ribbon.

His Highness wore a chrome-nickel-steel watch and stopwatch on his left wrist; he wore no rings.

His Highness got dressed within minutes, and left for the sortie in the best of spirits.

3. In what capacity did you go out to the wreckage of the plane?

3. I went out to the wreckage of the plane with Major General Vitéz László Szabó at around 1500 hours. His Highness's body had already been removed. The committee had in its possession and has shown me a watch and decoration ribbons, which I recognised and recognise with absolute certainty as belonging to His Highness. I am prepared to swear this on oath before any authority. I particularly know the watch because I bought it for His Highness a year ago, at his request, from Harpy in Budapest. The 9 mm Frommer repeating pistol which I have now been shown is just like one His Highness bought in the armaments factory in Hungary; I can find no distinguishing marks on the epaulette. On the basis of this evidence I am convinced that the body removed from the wreckage of the aeroplane and, on the committee's instructions and in my presence, placed in a coffin and taken away, was that of His Highness the Vice-Regent, Vitéz István Horthy de Nagybánya.

4. Do you have anything more to add?

4. I have nothing more to add.

The record was read aloud and then signed by way of confirmation.
Signature: György Farkas
Concluded at 2210 hours.
Date as above.
Signatures of committee members.

REMEMBERING
FLIGHT LT. STEPHEN HORTHY
BY THOSE WHO KNEW HIM WELL

Pál Álgyay-Hubert:
THE EMBODIMENT OF A MODERN ENGINEER

István Horthy was the living embodiment of a new breed of engineer which evolved during the course of the major reconstruction, restoration and modernisation works which were needed after the devastation of the first world war. A desire and a readiness to create characterised his whole life.

Even at the Technical University in Budapest his fellow engineering students were surprised and pleased to see that his was not the cool and condescending interest of someone set apart from the rest of society by reason of his origin, upbringing, and future. On the contrary, his work at the Technical University was characterised by a feverish interest in and the most thorough and exhaustive study of the subject, as well as the conscientiousness which became a hallmark of his subsequent career. But in addition to this, he made himself extremely popular and well-liked by taking a full part in the social life of the university in the students' Fraternal Society and by always associating with his colleagues in the most informal manner, with the familiarity of a friend.

The Technical University Amateur Flying Club elected him junior president in its most difficult period, because it expected him to be able to lead it out of its difficulties and successfully develop the sport of flying in Hungary.

He discussed and debated the club's affairs, leaving no stone unturned, and also found time to go down to the small workshop in the basement of the Technical

University, where he pored over detail drawings with a few young designers while a small group of skilled workers welded, filed, drilled, and built new aircraft fuselages and wings. It was then that he dedicated himself to the cause of aviation in Hungary; already acknowledged as an outstanding car driver and mechanical expert, he now began to fly as well, and his great talent, which would be admired the world over, began to develop.

Thus István Horthy set out on the road which signified the start of an epic period in Hungarian aviation, the dawning of a great future—the road which led ultimately to the great Hungarian tragedy: apotheosis in a heroic death.

During the time he spent studying in America, he got to the heart of mass production in the huge factory where he was working, in which every movement and every second had been tested and measured. In a few months he saw what was outdated and what should be developed in the eternally feverish relationship between man and his creations.

At the MÁVAG [*Magyar Állami Vas-, Acél- és Gépgyár—Hungarian Iron, Steel and Engineering Works*], a new engineering spirit entered the factory when he arrived. Ideas, action, and work flowed from him in an unending stream. It was here that his outstanding, sympathetic and altruistic creative spirit became apparent, a spirit to which all the staff and engineers working at MÁVAG at the time can attest.

We could all see and observe, we all knew that István Horthy was an engineer in the more noble, exalted and idealised sense of the word. He was not an expert of limited perspective, interested only in his own field, and with a tendency to get bogged down in details. He was an engineer who could see everything realistically and clearly, who could immediately get to the nub of a problem, who did not get lost in a mass of data, regulations, and long-winded definitions and descriptions, but could immediately cut through them to produce the truth, a precise statement formulated in the most concise, unambiguous, relevant, and accurate terms.

We were able to observe his lightning-quick and always unassailably certain powers of judgement in countless meetings, discussing the most varied problems. He never ever wavered in his judgement. He listened to all the arguments and ideas, but then formed his opinion completely independently, according to his own convictions.

He was also a natural engineer in that his manner with everybody was simple, confident, unflustered, calm and composed. He never became heated in an argument. As a result, he could appear reticent when people first met him or if they only saw him briefly. Those of us who knew him well and were able to admire his creative personality over a long period knew that he was likeable and friendly to everybody.

His fairness of thought and character were unparalleled. He personified the modern type of engineer: one who in the modern western countries plays a leading role in guiding almost all areas of state and public affairs.

We engineers looked forward to boundless opportunities, a bright future, advantages and prosperity for Hungary in general, but particularly in technical areas, since István Horthy, representing what was most outstanding in Hungarian engineering, was to assume a leading position here, where individuals with outstanding technical and other skills had not yet been given sufficient opportunity to prove their worth.

His status as Vice-Regent also led the engineering profession in Hungary to hope that its ambitions and readiness to participate in building the state would be fulfilled. Knowing that increasing areas of the government would be in his hands stimulated engineers' desire to create.

All these hopes have now been dashed. But in joining up for military service, in his life and behaviour at the front, his determination to fight, and his heroic death he also performed an unprecedentedly great and important mission and an incalculable service for his nation.

Everybody mourns him. We engineers, his closest colleagues, mourn him perhaps more than anyone else, because he was a great leader of Hungarian engineering.

(The author, Dr Pál Álgyay-Hubert, is a lecturer at the Technical University in Budapest. Formerly His Majesty's State Secretary for Transport, he is Vice-President of the Hungarian Transport Science Society.

The text is taken from "Vitéz nagybányai Horthy István élete és a magyar közlekedés" [*The life of Vitéz István Horthy de Nagybánya and Transport in Hungary*], edited by Olaf Wulff and Jenő Maleter; Budapest 1943, pp. 36–38.)

Jenő Markotay-Velsz:
THE DEPUTY MANAGING DIRECTOR OF THE STATE IRON WORKS

During the night of 19th–20th August 1942 something extraordinary happened which affected me for a long time and which I will never forget.

I slept very restlessly, and kept dreaming about our late Vice-Regent. Even now, I can almost hear the words he spoke to me in my dream: "Don't go thinking the Russians shot me down, I just crashed."

In the morning I woke up feeling very depressed. I tried to forget the bad dream, but it was impossible. It was in the afternoon that I heard the shocking news of this great tragedy, and I realised with alarm that in my dream I had experienced what had actually happened. This incident seemed incomprehensible, and the only explanation I can give for it is something I was once told by a very erudite Chinese gentleman.

The human body and soul are probably a big transmission centre which emits waves just as a radio broadcasting station does. But it can not just emit waves, it can also receive the waves transmitted by others. However, just as the transmitted waves can only be received on a radio receiver if it is set to the wavelength of the transmitted waves, so the human soul can only receive the messages transmitted by others if it is able to set itself to the same wavelength. The things which enable us to do this are a long time spent together with, and a true love and devotion for, the other person.

We worked together for seven years, and for six of these we shared an office. Our desks were next to each other, we had lunch together every day, and very often we did not part company until late at night. I have so many happy memories of this long period that I was very pleased and honoured to be asked by the Hungarian Transport Science Society to write a commemoration of Vitéz István Horthy de Nagybánya: the man, the engineer, the factory manager, and the leading expert on, enthusiastic supporter of, and tireless worker for transport and related issues.

His Majesty's Government appointed me managing director of the Magyar Királyi Állami Vas-, Acél- és Gépgyárak [*Hungarian State Iron, Steel and Engineering Works*] with effect from 1st January 1933. The next morning at 9 o'clock a three-man delegation from the MÁVAG branch of the Hungarian Technicians' Fraternal Society arrived, led by Vitéz István Horthy de Nagybánya, chief engineer in MÁVAG's car workshop and the society's branch leader, who welcomed me on behalf of the branch. I was moved by the devotion and affection he showed for the company, and could see that he cared deeply about the welfare of the factory and its employees. Shortly afterwards there was a branch meeting which he chaired. All the engineers in the factory were present. Here I could see that he was a born leader, and that the engineers liked and respected their young colleague very much. So in the interests of MÁVAG, which was in a critical situation, I appointed Vitéz István Horthy de Nagybánya to be deputy managing director and my closest colleague. I was touched by his protests that he was too young for the post and that he had not yet merited such a promotion. It took a lot of persuasion to convince him that the scope of a workshop engineer's duties was too narrow for someone with his abilities, and that he had to prepare himself for what Providence had called him to do. He had to get to know Hungarian economic life though direct experience, as with his talent, expertise, and hard work he would sooner or later have to take a leading role in it. That was when I first experienced his infinite modesty, one of his basic characteristics. Each time he was promoted, I had to reassure him again and again that he was not being promoted because he was the son of Hungary's Regent, and prove that he was being singled out on merit.

His modesty was rivalled by his disciplined behaviour. I have got to know many people in my life, but never one who was as disciplined as he was. He never sought his own comfort and knew no personal interests: all that mattered to him was to carry out the task he had been set. He was obliging and obedient to his superiors, and with his subordinates there was nothing he disapproved of more than undisciplined behaviour. He carried out instructions precisely, but was strict in demanding that his own instructions should also be carried out to the letter. He was never late, he never kept anyone waiting.

I am reminded of a little incident which characterises him best of all. One year the Regent's name-day fell on a Sunday and he was at Kenderes. He wanted to stay at Kenderes with his parents for lunch the next day, and he tried to phone me three times on Sunday to ask my permission. As it happened, I was away and he was unable to speak to me. On Monday morning he arrived punctually at the office.

He was incredibly conscientious and hard-working. He never spared himself if there was work that needed to be done. He frequently worked until late at night, and he was happy when he was working. His social obligations—and there were many of them—could not be considered while there was work to be done. The following incident illustrates this most eloquently. There was a gala performance at the Opera in honour of a guest from abroad. He had a phone call from the Regent's office to say that the Regent wanted him to attend as well. The performance started at 7 p.m., but István Horthy would not be sent away because he still had work to do. He hurried to the Opera at 9:30 in order to be there for the last act. He said it was more important to complete his work than to go to the opera.

Another incident: there was a meeting in Paris on a Thursday morning. On Tuesday he still had work to do in the factory, and could only travel on Wednesday. There was no aeroplane available. At 5 p.m. on Wednesday morning he left by car and drove all the way to Paris, arriving at 11 p.m.. All he had for lunch on the way was a ham roll he took with him.

His famous flight to India was also not a publicity stunt: he did it out of a sense of duty. To travel there and back by ship would have taken at least four weeks, and he did not want to be away that long, so he chose to fly in order to gain time. In seven years he took only three holidays of a fortnight each.

Nobody could compete with István Horthy in loyalty to his colleagues. He was with his fellow workers through thick and thin, and shared in all their worries and problems. It is well known that nowhere in the country was there such good team spirit as in the MÁVAG branch of the Hungaria Fraternal Society, of which he was not only the leader but the very soul. I will never forget the monthly meetings at which we fostered team spirit in the noblest sense. He never ever missed a meeting. In leading the meetings he was dignified, serious and decisive, but also kind, likeable, informal and easy-going; and listening to him was refreshing for the engineers who were tired after the hard day's work.

He was incredibly polite with everybody, but particularly with women. Few people were able to get to know his wonderfully gallant character as well as I did, and I can say that I have never in my life met a young man comparable to him in this regard. Once he was at my house, and when my six-year-old daughter entered the room, he stood up to greet her. My daughter was delighted and talked about this honour for a long time afterwards. Although he was basically reticent by nature, during the long time we spent together he did sometimes express his opinion on the fair sex, and this was so pure that such a noble, pure and chivalrous spirit perhaps last prevailed in the court of St. László. [*St. Ladislas, king of Hungary 1077–1095. He was very popular due to his heroic feats in driving out the nomadic Pechenegs (Cumans) who had been launching raids into Hungry.*]

But his best quality was the boundless love he showed his parents. It is impossible to put into words the charm, the respect, and the devotion he expressed in a few words of greeting to his mother. He looked up to his father as the most perfect man on Earth, and all he wanted was that his father should be pleased with him. Once he and I had an audience with His Highness the Regent in which we thanked him for the favour he had shown us in bestowing an honour on us. I looked with admiration at the boundless respect he showed to his father, and could see on his face the happiness which filled him at the thought that his father considered him worthy of an honour. The most eloquent illustration of this is the photograph taken of him on his return from his trip to India, as he hurried to greet his father. You could write volumes about his filial love, but words cannot express this noble emotion as faithfully as do István Horthy's expression and movements on that photograph.

However, István Horthy was not only called to be an example for millions to follow as a man; as an engineer he was also one of the best.

His knowledge of engineering, his skill, and his powers of judgement were amazing. He used all his spare time to increase his knowledge of engineering. With all the work he had to do, it was beyond me how he found the time to study technical books and periodicals. He had a keen interest in all branches of technology. He was an avid reader of technical reports—but he was not content with just reading the articles, he also strove to make use of anything of value in the factory. He would mark the article with yellow pencil and pass it on to the relevant person for him to read, and would then discuss it with him. But he was not just a man of theory: his practical knowledge and flair were also quite extraordinary. He frequently astonished a workshop engineer or worker by himself demonstrating how to do the job. More than once he came up from the workshop grimy and oily, reporting with pleasure that one or other of his experiments had been a success.

However, his real speciality was forms of transport and in particular the engine. He had a complete mastery of shipping and railways, both technically and in terms of transport, but with the engine he was definitely one of the country's leading experts. It was a pleasure to hear him debating with leading experts from abroad, and they in turn were amazed at his profound and thorough knowledge. He knew of all innovations, wherever they had occurred, and assessed them with a sure and relevant critique. Every year he attended the European motor shows, and absorbed all he saw and learned like a sponge.

As deputy managing director of MÁVAG, István Horthy dealt mainly with problems relating to forms of transport and to the manufacture of engines.

The task which had to be accomplished in 1933 was unbelievably difficult. MÁVAG, one of Hungary's largest factories, was in deep trouble. Its equipment was outdated and deficient, and it had no work to speak of. The company's locomotive factory was the only one in the country, but it was on the verge of closing down due to lack of orders. The first task was to prevent the locomotive factory from closing down completely. The government wanted to stop the manufacture of locomotives because of the deficit. Negotiations continued for months, and during the course of these negotiations István Horthy fought with youthful ardour and great enthusiasm for the maintenance of locomotive manufacture. But all this would have been to no avail if we had not been able to secure foreign orders for the locomotive workshop: István Horthy went to London, and as a result the first order—locomotive boilers for India—arrived. However, in Hungary the trend away from locomotives and towards motor cars continued. So the factory management decided to design a locomotive which would be able to compete with motor cars. Thus the first Hungarian streamlined locomotive was born, and István Horthy played a major part in its design and construction. He was delighted when the streamlined locomotive was ready, and often drove it himself on the test runs. He constantly held discussions with experts from MÁV [*Magyar Államvasutak—Hungarian State Railways*] about the design of new locomotives and the modernisation of old ones, and he was held in high regard by everyone for his expertise and tirelessness.

Car manufacture was in an even more desperate state in 1933. There were two car factories in Hungary, both without work. The two factories had about 400 lorries in stock, and sales in 1932 amounted to just twelve. In addition, MÁVAG's car works were completely outdated and ill-equipped, which made it impossible to produce cars economically. Thus the government was pressing MÁVAG to stop manufacturing cars completely. In order to prevent this, we needed on the one hand to build a new workshop, and on the other hand to sell the existing stock as soon as possible, and boost demand for lorries and buses.

Equipping the new car works was planned by István Horthy himself, as he had the most detailed knowledge of car manufacture. How happy he was when the arrival of a new machine tool was reported to him, how he could admire modern processing machines, and how enthusiastically he started them operating! Within a year the new car factory was complete, and its work increased so much that in six years it needed to be extended twice. I do not need to say just how much a productive, large car factory means to the country today.

However, we could not manufacture the old, outdated models in the new car factory: we had to change over to manufacturing modern cars. István Horthy provided a splendid solution to this problem. He negotiated tirelessly in Hungary and abroad, he worked extremely conscientiously, aware of his responsibility, on the difficult task of ensuring that we manufactured the most appropriate car for our circumstances. This was where he used his great expertise and experience to really good effect.

István Horthy's achievements in boosting road haulage are also outstanding. He negotiated constantly to sell the existing lorries, and it is entirely due to him that within a short time the four hundred lorries were boosting motor vehicle traffic in Hungary. On his initiative and with his encouragement, MATEOSZ [*Magyar Teherautó-Fuvarosok Országos Szövetsége—National Association of Road Hauliers of Hungary*] put the lorries held in stock on the road: he found a way of enabling small businessmen to obtain lorries. Hungarian car factories and hauliers owe him an eternal debt of gratitude.

At the time of the economic crisis in 1933 MÁVAG's iron and steel works in Diósgyőr were under threat as well. Their principal output was railway building materials—rails, points, and crossings. Orders had to be obtained from abroad. A great opportunity for this arose in the winter of 1933–34 in connection with railway building works in Persia. Direct negotiations were needed, and somebody had to travel to Teheran. István

Horthy readily volunteered to do the job. I did not want to let him go, I did not want it to be him who had to travel through Russia. When I saw that his mind was made up, I wanted at least to send an engineer with him so that he would not have to make the long and dangerous journey alone. He did not want to take anybody with him, because he considered it unnecessary as well as expensive for the company. He spent six weeks in Teheran, gained a great deal of experience, and made MÁVAG a well-known and respected name. Years later the manager of a large French concern stated that they had made a very costly mistake in not recognising early enough the threat that István Horthy's negotiations in Teheran posed to them.

MÁVAG exported a great deal of railway rolling stock to the British colonies, particularly India. István Horthy undertook the organisation of these shipments, and it was in order to do this that he flew to India. He made the long journey alone, without an escort, in his small private plane - a sporting achievement which is almost unique. He completed his task in India with complete success, and it was only the outbreak of war which prevented MÁVAG from enjoying the fruits of his labours.

István Horthy represented the company countless times in negotiations abroad, and wherever he went he was conspicuous for being extremely well informed and well prepared. He prepared conscientiously for all negotiations, studying the material days beforehand: not even the smallest, least significant item escaped his notice. He was a permanent member of the International Rail Cartel, in which he frequently fought with the utmost vigour to defend the interests of Hungarian factories.

Almost single-handedly he started up aircraft manufacture in Hungary. The development of aircraft manufacture encountered difficulties and obstacles so severe that anyone else would have been unable to overcome them. The task of starting up aircraft manufacture on a large scale was beset by constraints which only István Horthy was able to tackle. He started this major task with youthful ardour and firm conviction, and we could not but admire the enthusiasm, the tenacity, and the persistence with which he achieved his aim. He was constantly negotiating, calling meetings, receiving and leading delegations, until he succeeded in getting the two factories involved in the manufacture of aircraft. He knew instinctively that the Hungarian army would only be able to carry out its duties in the coming ordeal if the aeroplane, the most up-to-date weapon, was available to it, and he saw clearly that Hungary could only occupy its rightful place among the cultured nations if it could become suitably involved in transport which was increasingly shifting into the air. This firm conviction, together with his ardent patriotism, gave István Horthy the strength and persistence to lay the foundations of aircraft manufacture in Hungary. The eagerness with which he served the cause of aviation is illustrated by the fact that one afternoon he took the factory engineers out to Buda's airport and took them each for a ten-minute flight. In this way he wanted to give them a liking for flying and win them over to the cause.

István Horthy carried out all these tasks, each of which could occupy a member of staff full-time, in addition to taking a full part, with a great sense of vocation, in the top-level management of a large factory in which very many problems arose.

My heart aches when I think how many hours of anxiety and how much worry he had to experience in order not just to preserve the crisis-ridden company, but to develop it and enable it to fulfil the great tasks the future would bring. Those were hard times! We could not choose which orders to take but constantly had to search for opportunities to obtain work. And if an opportunity arose to win an order, István Horthy threw all his energy into winning the work for MÁVAG. At times like that he did not spare himself. He went through the calculations again and again, he studied the financial situation and discussed manufacturing procedures, and was always ready to visit personally all those on whom the order depended.

He was not destined to enjoy the fruits of this tiring and stressful work, a time when the murderous price war and ferocious struggle between factories to win work would end—and how he longed for this time, and what plans he made for it! He took part in the hard work of sowing, but could not enjoy the happiness of the harvest.

God has many secrets which we may never be able to explain. The life and death of our Vice-Regent is probably one such secret, since human understanding cannot fathom how it is possible for someone to live his life as though he knows he does not have much time on Earth and has to hurry in order to become worthy of apotheosis in the short time available. We cannot help believing that God intended him to be a model for all Hungarians, to show the people he passionately loved the road on which they must travel in order to arrive.

(The author, Vitéz Jenő Markotay-Velsz, is a chief government advisor and managing director of the Hungarian State Iron, Steel and Machine Works [MÁVAG].

The text is taken from "Vitéz nagybányai Horthy István élete és a magyar közlekedés" [*The Life of Vitéz István Horthy de Nagybánya and Transport in Hungary*], edited by Olaf Wulff and Jenő Maleter; Budapest 1943, pp. 89–96.)

Kálmán Imrédy:
ISTVÁN HORTHY AS PRESIDENT OF THE STATE RAILWAYS

I can still see the young, dashing figure of Vitéz István Horthy de Nagybánya as he stood before me on the occasion when, I welcomed him with great pleasure on behalf of the board of the State Railways to the post of president. And individual episodes of my contacts with him in the feverish pace of day-to-day work as well as the memorable incidents of his life—from the splendid celebration of his election as Vice-Regent to the moving and very sad concluding ceremony of his earthly career as he was placed in the crypt in Kenderes—are projected like fleeting images onto the white screen of my memory.

It is indeed difficult to think of him and remember him without being deeply moved and saddened.

He had embarked on a career in the navy, and when that became impossible, he changed over to mechanical engineering. After graduating in mechanical engineering, he spent a short time working in the aircraft department of the Csepel engineering works, and then continued his practical studies in Ford's Detroit works, where he spent a whole year, initially as an ordinary worker. On his return he was appointed deputy head of the bus department of the MÁVAG [*Magyar Állami Vas-, Acél- és Gépgyárak—Hungarian State Iron, Steel and Engineering Works*], and later he became the factory's deputy managing director and managing director. In this position, making full use of his earlier practical experience, he established new and dynamic working practices which greatly increased output. But even while he was fully occupied with his studies and then with his work as an engineer, he still found time to pursue his favourite sports intensively, which he continued doing with his fit physique and youthful enthusiasm right up to his heroic death. At a very early age his restlessly working nature became apparent: he always wanted to create, to advance. His life was movement, and his living space was everywhere where it was possible to move, to travel, to advance. This preference led him towards sports which involved movement, whether this occurred on water, on land, or in the air; and he was equally interested in sailing, car driving, the railways, and air transport. The profound and vivid impressions made on the young man by the feverishly busy, multi-faceted life of the naval base at Pola exerted a great influence on the development of his personality and inclinations. The impressions he gained there matured by the time he reached manhood into an irresistible longing for sports and activities which involved movement. Thus he became an outstanding rider, an enthusiastic driver, a pilot with endurance and without fear; and thus he came to occupy a significant and responsible management position in a major transport company: that of president of the Royal Hungarian State Railways.

He came from the most exalted circles to head the Royal Hungarian State Railways, an institution which was democratic in the noblest sense of the word, in which he had to deal with the destinies and vital problems of people ranging from the highest officials to the lowliest workers. As an expert he took up his post equipped with first-class theoretical qualifications, a very lively and healthy flair for economics, and a great deal of wide-ranging practical experience obtained in various positions and on various continents. But he was also receptive to the vital problems of ordinary workers struggling to make ends meet. Thus he was predestined by reason both of his intellectual qualifications and of his character to lead the country's biggest company.

He came to us very modestly, but having prepared conscientiously for the great task, ready to place all his expertise, his energy, his powers of judgement, his sense of responsibility, his dedication, and the noble virtue of fulfilling his duty, at the service of the task he had been set. He came and conquered! He won everybody over with his smooth, obliging and polite manner. He always assessed and recognised each person's expertise, opinions and views with the utmost objectivity, thereby gaining everyone's sincere respect and loyalty. With his decisive and clear instructions and his quick, sound and wise decisions he gained everyone's esteem; and with his altruism, his great desire to help, and the effective aid he gave to those of his colleagues in need who turned to him, he won people's hearts. The steps he took to achieve greater economies led to the State Railways returning a significant trading profit for the first time after many years of losses. He did everything in the unpretentious and natural manner which is a quality that only great minds and great intellects possess.

He took up the post of president on 1st June 1940, and was welcomed particularly warmly at the next business managers' meeting by the minister József Varga. He came to us at a time when the current gigantic world conflict was already in progress, and some of the preliminaries had already been completed. During his term of office the country made its third welcome territorial gain. These exceptional events placed almost unimaginable transport demands on the State Railways. Our rolling stock was barely sufficient for normal peacetime traffic, and we had to continue this in addition to taking on the very sensitive and onerous task of providing for a significant volume of extra traffic. We had to start the process of repairing the neglected lines in the territories we had regained, we had to meet as far as possible the wishes of an extremely sensitive population which, having returned after much suffering in 23 years of oppression, wanted good services and connections—and all this without having regained sufficient coaches or locomotives with the northern and sub-Carpathian territories, and having regained none of either with the eastern territories and Transylvania. The renewed periods of territorial gain meant that the State Railways were faced with increasing personnel problems. With our limited staff we had to carry on rail traffic without interruption on a significantly increased network of lines, and at the same time we also had to carry out the difficult task of grading the staff transferred from foreign governments. With the territorial gains and changes of government, more and more tariff problems arose; transit, internal, and external traffic increased greatly; civil passenger and freight transport also increased due to a temporary decrease or interruption in the use of other forms of transport. Repairing and adding to our stock of locomotives and coaches tested our technical capabilities severely, and the provision of financial resources was also an unresolved problem. As a result of the state of war and increased consumption, procurement became much more difficult, which forced us to be much more attentive and prudent. With the armed reoccupation of part of the Bácska and southern regions in the spring of 1941 our workload and our problems increased even more. The most telling illustration of the proportionate increase in workload for the State Railways and their managers, and primarily for the president of the board, is provided by figures which show that during the time Vitéz István Horthy de Nagybánya was president the length of track operated by MÁV increased from 9326 km to 12,742 km.

New and bigger problems arose in addition to the multitude of everyday tasks and duties. One such major problem was that lines of communication in Transylvania had been cut in half, leaving the Székelyföld [*Szekler region*] without a rail connection to the main body of Hungary's railway system. The first step in remedying this was the building of a new narrow-gauge line between Szászlekence [*Lechinta*] and Kolozsnagyida [*Viile Tecii*], which provided Marosvásárhely [*Tirgu-Mures*] and the surrounding areas with a connection—if only a narrow-gauge one—to our main lines. Special bus and lorry services were introduced as a temporary measure between Szeretfalva [*Saratel*] and Szászrégen [*Reghin*]. The rapid building of the section of main line between Szerétfalva and Déda was a major technical project in terms of its scale, its conception, and the amount of money invested in it; from an economic, railway policy and strategic point of view its significance was almost incalculable, and it was a problem which had to be solved urgently due to circumstances which are well known. Preparing plans, inviting tenders, and letting the contracts were all significant tasks. Each stage involved extensive negotiations, discussions, and decisions of various kinds, requiring a great deal of energy. The plans were prepared from the ideas and conceptions of the late prime minister Count Pál Teleki and the trade and transport minister József Varga; unfortunately he did not live to see the completion of the works started on the basis of these plans.

István Horthy stood at the centre of this kaleidoscopic mass of tasks with his youthful and inexhaustible energy, cheerful and good-humoured. He took his full share in each task without flagging and with exemplary conscientiousness. He was interested in every issue, he gave guidance and made decisions. Nothing of any importance or significance escaped his notice. He was interested in all technical innovations, and strove to establish them within the State Railways, in order to keep the railways up-to-date in every respect. He took the lead in fulfilling his duties: he was an example to everyone—nobody could compete with him in diligence, reliability, or workload. Despite having a post which occupied him full-time, he did not become a narrow specialist. He maintained his interest in all forms of transport. The question of co-operation between the railways and the road hauliers was regulated again during the time he was president of MÁV. With his thorough knowledge of the issues, he was able to bring about full co-operation and ensure complete harmony between MÁV and MATEOSZ. He was a member of the board of directors of the Magyar Királyi Folyam- és Tengerhajózási Részvénytársaság [*Royal Hungarian River and Sea Shipping Company*], and planned to develop close co-operation between the Hungarian State Railways and the Royal Hungarian River and Sea Shipping Co. He was a member of the inter-state committee set up to settle the affairs of the Duna-Száva-Adria Vasuttársaság [*Danube-Sava-Adriatic Railway Company*], of the executive committee of the Central European Travel Bureau (MER), of IBUSZ [*the Hungarian state travel agency*], and many other transport bodies. He also did not neglect the cause of aviation, his favourite hobby, and was president of the Magyar Aero Szövetség [*Hungarian Aero Society*], and the Horthy Miklós Nemzeti Repülő Alap [*Horthy Miklós National Flying Foundation*]. He also dealt intensively with the issue of links between MÁV and aviation.

    He was a genuine transport expert and considered it vital to practice and develop the science of transport and promote disciplined scientific thought in the area of transport—to the extent that he worked with enthusiastic dedication to promote the formation of our society, the Magyar Közlekedéstudományi Társaság [*Hungarian Transport Science Society*]. With his support for the cause, the foundations of the society were laid. But he did not only honour our society with moral support, he made an intellectual contribution as well with papers published in the technical literature. He published two papers, "Az államvasutak és a nehézipar" [*The State Railways and Heavy Industry*] and "Közlekedési problémák tudományos megvilágításban" [*Transport Problems in a Scientific Light*], in the journal "Magyar Közlekedési Szemle" *[Hungarian Transport Review]*. In the latter paper he identified three issues of great importance for the society to debate exhaustively and in detail: the problem of Budapest's railway termini, already the subject of much debate; the question of a canal between the Danube and the Tisza; and issues relating to the determination of a new network of motorways in central Europe. The speech he made at a commemoration of Széchényi in Szolnok on 23rd November 1941 also appeared in "Magyar Közlekedési Szemle." [*István Széchényi, called 'the greatest Hungarian,' was a liberal statesman who proposed a variety of radical reforms, including the abolition of feudal land ownership. He founded the Academy of Sciences in 1825; among other activities, he supported the development of shipping on the Danube, and he was responsible for the building of the Chain Bridge in Budapest between 1842 and 1848 as well as for flood prevention works on the Tisza and Danube rivers.*] In a profound analysis he presented Széchényi as a political realist, stating that if the country wanted to be successful, then we had to move along the path based on reality which Széchényi had marked out. This work, in which he declares that Széchényi is his model and hero, marks his emergence as an expert and masterly practitioner of the science of transport. Our society was simply showing its sincere respect and affection and expressing its deep gratitude to him when, after his election as Vice-Regent, it elected him the society's patron by acclamation.

When he became a member of the upper house for the county of Jász-Nagykun-Szolnok our suspicions were renewed, and we could not help thinking that those who were in charge of our country's destiny at the highest level intended him to take on a more important and responsible role. Subsequent events confirmed our suspicions, and when both houses of the Hungarian Parliament unanimously elected him Vice-Regent on 19th February 1942, though we were very pleased at his appointment to this high office, we had to acknowledge that he would leave his post as chairman of MÁV, and our company would lose the outstanding character, the intellectual and moral values of this man for whom we had such affection.

From that day he outwardly ceased to be a railwayman, and the varied and wide-ranging duties which constituted his work as chairman of MÁV were replaced by the new, richer and more colourful duties of government. Unfortunately these duties left very little room for the cause of the railways or transport in general. However, in his heart he remained a railwayman, and as a result of his experiences as chairman of our company, he always spoke with the utmost warmth and appreciation of the company and its staff, even in his exalted position. When he took his leave of us, he promised to maintain his interest in the company in the future, and said that we could count on him in all major issues. We can now only guess at the affection in this promise, and the effect it could have had on the future development of the State Railways.

Vitéz István Horthy de Nagybánya was a bright guiding star on the horizon of transport. He came, and departed suddenly. His was a great promise which due to the wishes of higher authorities could not be fulfilled; he was not destined to become another Széchényi or Gábor Baross in the service of transport. [*Gábor Baross was Minister of Public Works and Transport between 1886 and 1889; he founded the Hungarian State Railways.*]

We stand, moved and deeply saddened, before the great mystery of God's unfathomable will. There is nothing we can do! Vitéz István Horthy has died a hero's death and is no more, but his glorious memory lives on and will live on forever. I think the most beautiful and fitting tribute to him would be to quote the marvellous words the poet János Arany wrote about his hero, István Széchényi: "He does not die who spends on millions / the treasure of his rich life, though his day may pass; / but having shaken off what is earthly in him, / he is purified into a life-giving idea, / which remains, its clear light always growing, / as it moves away in time and space; / to which the successor's virtue looks up: / desires, hopes, believes and prays."

(The author, Dr Kálmán Imrédy de Omorovicza, is president of the board of MÁV, and vice-president of the Hungarian Transport Science Society.

The text is taken from "Vitéz Nagybányai Horthy István élete és a magyar közlekedés" [*The Life of Vitéz István Horthy de Nagybánya and Transport in Hungary*], edited by Olaf Wulff and Jenő Maleter; Budapest 1943, pp. 116–121.)

István Eszláry:
IN THE PRESIDENT'S OFFICE

As I pick up my pen, I am deeply aware of the tragedy of my situation: it is I who have to write a commemoration of him, when I was almost two decades older than him. If it ever flashed through my mind during the years of intense work which I was able to spend at his side that we would one day be parted, then I imagined him accompanying me, his faithful old squire, on my final journey. But fate decreed otherwise. Deeply moved, I will try to describe the kind of person he was in the office, and the effect of his personality on his working environment and on all those with whom he came into contact through work.

It was through sport that I first met him. My first impressions of him go back to the very early 1920s. He used to go as a youth member, with his younger brother Miklós, to Hungaria Evezős Egyesület [*Hungaria Rowing Club*] boathouse—which at that time was fairly old and cramped—on Margaret Island in Budapest. He did not just attend training sessions regularly, but sometimes also took part in day-long boat trips. Such trips, on which the young rowers enjoyed themselves without the least inhibition, gave me an excellent opportunity to observe the young István Horthy's character. He was kind and good-humoured, but was always able to hold back from frivolity. If the company's high spirits tended towards over-exuberance, he tactfully held back from their excesses. On such occasions too he would always speak to his older club-mates—after all he and his brother were the youngest in the group—in a polite and disciplined manner. For a long time after that our paths crossed only rarely and for a few minutes at a time. It was only on the board of the State Railways that I was once again in constant close proximity to him. I was there in the board room in the last days of May 1940, when the departing president of the board of MÁV introduced to him as new president the chief officials of the company, his future colleagues. He gave everyone a serious, searching glance and a warm, manly handshake. With this handshake he seemed to be making an agreement with each one of us on the work we would be starting together. Even then he captivated us all with his calm, confident demeanour, his kind manner, and his handsome appearance. You couldn't imagine a finer, more handsome young man. As I saw his slim figure walk along the line of those welcoming him, I was reminded of an old song glorifying the 11th century Hungarian king St László [*St. Ladislas—see note earlier*], a paragon of chivalry—the song might have been about István Horthy.

However, after the brief welcoming ceremony, he got down to work at once; and work started at a pace which could only be imagined close to István Horthy. I had been office manager to the president of the Board of the State Railways for many years, and he had enough confidence in me to keep me on in this post. I was an old hand, having served two previous presidents of the State Railways in this capacity. Both of these had been old and outstanding officials, not only excellent as transport officials in Hungary, but also well known and highly regarded in their field throughout Europe. However, István Horthy—a new president and a new man in transport policy—very rapidly gained a firm grasp of all the significant issues in MÁV, this enormous company, and within weeks it had become apparent that he was a most worthy successor to his illustrious predecessors. He had an excellent understanding of the issues. He could see at once what was significant in terms of the company's performance and business results and needed his firm control, and what only came to the president through office formalities or habit: the latter were put aside. However, anything he recognised as significant or considered important for his own information he took firmly in hand, and was interested in the most minute details. Anyone who reported to him on such a matter really had to know his subject, because in the right place and at the right time he could be very firm and resolute, even obstinate.

In this way, without wasting his attention and energy on insignificant matters, he had a thorough and precise knowledge of everything of significance concerning MÁV. On the basis of this precise and thorough information, his sharp powers of judgement immediately formed a firm verdict, an unerring and correct decision. I can say that whenever he made an authoritative decision as president of MÁV on significant issues relating to the company, it was the right one; and he was in his element making decisions on difficult, but at the same time often fine and very interesting problems. In general his whole mental outlook was that of a true and ideal large company head who is inseparable from his company, and while he was at the head of MÁV, almost all he thought about was serving the great institution which had been placed in his charge, and the enormous national interests linked to it.

At this point I would like to mention his sense of duty. Anyone who, as he did, felt completely at one with the institution placed in his charge, could do nothing other than deal constantly with MÁV's problems, talk about them, discuss them, receive reports and make decisions from morning till night, whether in the office or in the car driving home, or even while travelling by train.

But he was not satisfied with the fact that he himself was filled with a sense of duty. He considered it important to transplant this firm sense of duty into his surroundings, so he made sure that his sense of duty was outwardly apparent, so that on seeing this, first and foremost those who worked close to him, but at the same time all employees of MÁV, should be aware of their duty. And everyone around him worked with the utmost orderliness and punctuality. The president's office staff had to be ready and waiting for him each morning to present reports, with all the material assembled with the utmost care. And during the day if he had a minute's break from receiving reports or interviewing people, he would immediately come across to my room—a distance of perhaps three paces—and ask if I had anything new to report, if any urgent reports had come in, or if there was any new information in those matters which particularly interested him at the time. In general he much preferred direct, verbal discussions, and taking action in relation to these as quickly as possible. He was not a man to pore over files for any length of time. He considered documents necessary only to put on record the most essential facts: he did not like to spend a long time scribbling things down, but much preferred to hear submissions from the people themselves, because that way he saw them face to face and could see into them.

He spent both morning and afternoon in the office. Though his elevated social position brought with it social engagements as well, he kept these to a minimum. During the two years I spent in close proximity to him, there were very few days when he was not in the office from morning till night, and on the rare occasions when he was not, this was usually due to an engagement even greater or more important that his work.

He was almost always sitting in his office by five o'clock in the afternoon. And as he usually called me in as soon as he arrived, I had to take good care to arrive at least a quarter of an hour before him, so that I could prepare my reports properly.

He would work until eight or nine at night. When he finished his work, he would come across to me with his usual friendly smile. As I generally made use of the quiet time in the evening—when the telephones no longer disturbed me—to do those jobs which required a little peace and quiet, he usually asked me, and often looked at, what I was doing. Then—as there were no buses at that time of night—he would offer to take me home. The car naturally took him home to the Castle first, and then took me to my flat in Buda. However, more than once he had dismissed his official car in the afternoon, and it was his own car which was parked outside the gate. On these occasions—despite all my protests—he would first drive me all the way home before driving home himself.

I would briefly describe the general atmosphere around him in the office as one of true cordiality in the midst of the utmost discipline, seriousness and hard work.

I could write whole chapters on how well he could deal with people on formal and informal occasions. He could capture the hearts of ordinary people for ever with a few kind words. He knew exactly the right tone to adopt with the person facing him; and if he was with foreigners, during negotiations he was the one who was absolutely certain of what he wanted and, without losing sight of it for a moment, generally achieved it. However, over dinner after the official negotiations he was the most amiable and witty conversationalist.

He avoided all ostentation, and kept himself out of the public eye as far as possible, even if people's interest was the sincere admiration which a heroic feat always provokes in people. An incident which took place on a hot day in the summer of 1941 is typical. He had been in the office from early in the morning until half past two, and as his family was not in Budapest, he went to one of the baths in the early afternoon to have lunch and refresh himself. But he was back in his office, as he always was, before five o'clock, and started his usual afternoon jobs without a word. I had just finished submitting my usual afternoon report to him when journalists started ringing me and his secretary and then arrived in person. They told us that in the baths our president had at the last moment saved a swimmer who had got into difficulties from certain death, and having brought him out of the water, quickly went to his cabin, got changed, and left immediately. They were only able to catch up with him here, and wanted a brief interview about his life-saving act. When we reported this to our president, he refused the request, and instructed me to ask the journalists not to write a word about the incident. They complied.

If he took a short afternoon break, this was only in the summer; the winter was a succession of grey days filled with continuous work. He knew no rest, and even refused invitations to go hunting. To my knowledge he only went hunting once in the two years, and that was an official engagement.

However, he loved his work all the more. He often said how much he enjoyed his work at the MÁV. And his every act showed that this was so, because you could not imagine an area of work better suited to his personality than the post of president of MÁV in these stormy times. Difficult and interesting problems arose one after the other: no sooner had he made a decision on one problem than he had to form an opinion on another. And this suited his work-hungry nature, his lively, restless spirit, and his excellent, quick, sure and keen sense of judgement very well.

His heroic death was deeply distressing to the country; all strata of Hungarian society were united in their grief. But however direct and moving the outward signs of general grief were, I am firmly convinced that Hungary still does not know what it lost with the death of Vitéz István Horthy. He would have been a sea wall firm enough to break every wave of these stormy times.

(The author, Dr. István Eszláry de Tiszaföldvár, is a chief government advisor, deputy director of MÁV, and former head of the Vice-Regent's secretariat.

The text is taken from "Vitéz Nagybányai Horthy István élete és a magyar közlekedés" [*The Life of Vitéz István Horthy de Nagybánya and Transport in Hungary*], edited by Olaf Wulff and Jenő Maleter; Budapest 1943, pp. 136–141.)

György Segesváry:
THE FIRST VOLUNTEER PILOT

Vitéz István Horthy de Nagybánya was not quite a year older than me. While we were still in Vienna we both decided that we would join the navy. He got into the naval academy in Pola a year before me; I was to follow him there in the following year. But he dissuaded me from going because of the first world war, and in fact he himself returned home from Pola in circumstances which are well known.

Our childhood friendship continued here in Budapest after His Highness the Regent started his military service. We were both very keen on sport, particularly motor sports: motorcycles, and later cars. As my estate bordered on the crown estate near Gödöllő we were always together at sporting, hunting and other events organised by landowners and others in the area. Our friendship was strengthened by the fact that while we were at school, we were almost always honourable opponents in motorbike, car, and skiing races, except possibly for one occasion when our current special ambassador, Miklós Horthy jr., was my opponent and Pista [*abbreviation of István*] my partner in a tennis match.

After completing secondary school I studied at the agricultural college in Keszthely, where I became president of the students' union and thereby junior president of the college, and Miklós Horthy jr., who was a year below me, became vice-president and then succeeded me after my graduation. During our student years too we were often together during the winter as well as the summer in an intimate circle of friends or at sporting or other social events, for which István Horthy would also travel down. He and I were both close to completing our studies when on a spring day we decided that Hungarian aviation was hamstrung and we had to do something to restore to young Hungarians the opportunity to fly. Naturally we both first had to obtain our parents' consent; and we both found that our fathers agreed much more readily than our mothers. With the wise and well-intentioned support of the high-ranking military leaders of the time, we managed to enlist—though secretly—as the first volunteers in Hungary's post-Trianon air force. István Horthy went straight to Szombathely, while I later followed a trial plan secretly developed by the Defence Ministry and went first to one of the artillery units, then to a course on rapid revolution engines, and then to the pilot school in Szombathely. István Horthy as a brevet bombardier was the highest-ranking member of the first year, and I as a brevet chief gunner was the lowest-ranking member. Since the year group consisted of only two men, in the infantry drill sessions our instructor would very often use canes to represent additional men in order to illustrate formation changes which required more than two men. During our training we never received any favours or preferential treatment of any kind.

The future Vice-Regent did all the hardest and dirtiest repair and maintenance work with as much enthusiasm and dedication as the strenuous infantry drill or any theoretical subject. We got up at around 3 o'clock in the morning and hardly stopped until sunset. We would go into town once or twice a week, and then only to buy basic necessities. Apart from the trainees and the instructors, nobody knew that the Regent's son was there. We completed our training in Szeged, where our treatment was similar to the treatment we had received in Szombathely.

Vitéz István Horthy's behaviour during the whole time we were together was military and disciplined. Some minor lapses of general discipline did occur, for which all the trainees were punished as a group, but he naturally took the punishment with the rest. He had no subordinates at that time, since he himself was only a junior aviation assistant, but because of his quick wits, his skill, his great ability to grasp situations, and his polite but military manner he was very popular with everyone. If there was a job for which volunteers were required, he would always volunteer, and he was very unhappy if anyone tried to treat him differently out of consideration for his origins. He was a sensible, calm, level-headed and circumspect pilot.

When we had completed our year as volunteers, the first thing he did was to push his case in the appropriate quarters as a precedent in order to open the way for young Hungarians who wanted to fly. As a result, in 1928 a modest squad of volunteers joined the pilots: this has grown each year, and now provides an enormous impetus and support for young people who want to fly.

After completing his college course, despite being very busy, he still found the time to devote himself to the cause of aviation in Hungary, and with his increasing influence he supported and set up one flourishing youth flying club after another. Sometimes we talked until late at night about these plans, sketching out the opportunities in glowing terms, and going over the problems and how to avoid them. He never stopped working on this until the day he died, showing an example with his personal life to the young people of Hungary.

(The author, György Segesváry de Segesvár, has responsibility for air transport in the Hungarian Royal Trade and Transport Ministry. The text is taken from "Vitéz Nagybányai Horthy István élete és a magyar közlekedés" [*The Life of Vitéz István Horthy de Nagybánya and Transport in Hungary*], edited by Olaf Wulff and Jenő Maleter; Budapest 1943, pp. 242–243.)

Rezső Laborczffy:
ISTVÁN HORTHY'S ACHIEVEMENTS IN CIVILIAN AVIATION

I first met Vitéz István Horthy de Nagybánya in May 1928, when we organised the Hungarian Aero Club's flying day at the Mátyásföld airfield, in order to promote flying. I got to know him better later on, in 1936, when we organised international pilots' reunions, and after 1938, when he became president of the Hungarian Aero Society and then of the Horthy Miklós National Flying Foundation, and honoured me by choosing me to work with him. I was co-president with him of the Aero Society and his deputy in the Horthy Miklós Flying Foundation.

On the Mátyásföld flying day Vitéz István Horthy—as the first and only volunteer pilot—was part of a team which was to put on an aerobatics display for the public in the presence of His Highness the Regent. At that time Hungarian aviation was still in its infancy and the stunts performed in the display—looping the loop, rolling, and flying upside down—were manoeuvres which very few amateur pilots could perform.

It would have been excellent publicity for the flying day if we had been able to announce that Vitéz István Horthy, son of the Regent, would perform in an aerobatics display. However, he did not allow us to publicise this. Since we could not publicise the names of the air force officers taking part due to the terms of the Trianon peace treaty, we could not publicise his name either. He did not want to be an exception when his fellow pilots were performing anonymously.

During the following years, when the Hungarian Touring Club organised international pilots' reunions ("pilots' picnics") in Hungary, I was commander of the Székesfehérvár air base and also had responsibility for the airfield at Balatonkiliti, near Siófok, where the main events of the international pilots' reunions took place.

In official circles this international event received only moral support. If Vitéz István Horthy had not taken the trouble to go there personally beforehand to discuss the organisation and persuade the appropriate local authorities to take the necessary steps, then this first international pilots' reunion would also have been the last in Hungary.

I can clearly remember his encouraging words to us in connection with the difficulties of organising this event: "Remember that we are doing this for the cause of Hungary and Hungary's reputation. The emphasis is not on having a good time but on convincing these influential and important gentlemen from abroad that the Hungarian people are not only welcoming hosts but also keep order and discipline in the country. They should get to know us as we really are, not as we are described in Little Entente propaganda. Please support this cause." Well, we gave such support to the cause of the pilots' reunion over and above the officially prescribed moral support that in the years preceding the war they wanted to hold every international pilots' picnic in Hungary.

In 1938 I was on the committee which on behalf of the Defence Minister asked Vitéz István Horthy—who at that time was deputy managing director of MÁVAG—to accept the office of president of the Hungarian Aero Society. As a result of the Trianon Peace Treaty it was very important for Hungarian military aviation that the Hungarian Aero Society should function properly. István Horthy unselfishly and generously undertook to do his share of the work, but recommended that we appoint someone else as president rather than him. It was only after repeated official requests that he was prepared to accept the office, subject to the following conditions:

1. The government would provide the resources needed for the task, because—he said—it was only through planned and consistent work with the necessary financial backing that anything useful and lasting could be achieved for the country.

2. He could choose his colleagues himself, because he could only expect to be successful if he could appoint appropriate experts to head each area of work.

3. In addition, in order to accept the office of president, he needed the permission of the minister to whom he was responsible and of his father the Regent. As a state employee, he could only accept any outside work with the permission of his superiors, even if this was voluntary work which would not be detrimental to his service with MÁVAG.

Fortunately for the cause of aviation in Hungary, all his conditions were met.

The generous and outstanding work he did for the Hungarian Aero Society is well known. The public could see for themselves the results of his work at the public examination of civilian pilots held each year at Budaörs airport.

Later, having organised the Aero Society, he resigned the presidency and became president of the Horthy Miklós National Flying Foundation. Here too, he placed each area of work in the hands of suitable experts, and until he was convinced that their work was progressing in what he considered the right direction, he personally gave them detailed instructions, checked and corrected them - while at the same time he was managing director of the biggest state factory, and subsequently president of MÁV.

Under his personal direction and supervision civilian

and recreational aviation were organised, the necessary training framework was set up, and the required equipment was obtained and buildings were constructed. His capacity for work was astonishing; but just as he did not spare himself, he did not tolerate a lack of discipline and order around him. I was present at many negotiations in which he took part, and admired the speed with which he grasped the essential points of each problem. He quickly and painlessly disembarked from his ship those who prevaricated and those self-important gentlemen who made themselves out to be irreplaceable experts. He always listened to opposing views and well-grounded suggestions, and if he was convinced by the arguments, he adopted them; if not, he insisted on his decisions being implemented in full.

His former subordinates could speak volumes about his kindness and altruistic nature. He listened to all requests, and if he considered them justified, he did everything in his power to meet them.

In the early spring of 1939 Vitéz István Horthy was invited to London with other leading Hungarian pilots. At that time he was deputy managing director of MÁVAG and president of the Hungarian Aero Society, and could not be away for as long as it would take to travel to London and back by train. So he decided that he and his companions would make the journey by aeroplane. The weather conditions forecast along their route were not favourable, but he still insisted on leaving at the appointed time. The airport at Buda's was blanketed in fog, and the passenger planes were unable to take off. But when the first passenger plane took off for Vienna, Vitéz István Horthy left for London in his single-engine, 100 horse power private plane, which was not equipped with a radio. The airport authorities objected, saying that there was still low fog over the Danube, but he replied that he could fly over the clouds. Soon after taking off, one of those accompanying him, the transatlantic pilot Sándor Magyar, who was flying below the clouds, was forced to land on the Danube due to the fog. Despite the bad weather, Vitéz István Horthy flew to London and back according to plan.

On 18th July 1939, as deputy managing director of MÁVAG, he flew to Bombay and back in a 100 horse power private plane without radio equipment on an urgent business mission. He would have had to wait five days for the departure of a Dutch passenger plane, but the urgency of his business required him to leave at once. He covered 12,860 km in seven and a half days: the journey to Bombay took four days, and back to Budapest three and a half days. The Dutch airliner, which had two engines of 1000 horse power each, two pilots, a radio operator, and a mechanic, made the same journey in three days.

This achievement attracted the attention of aviation circles all over the world. I think the above details are sufficient for transport experts; any further explanation is superfluous. But I do think it is necessary to note that István Horthy's sensational flight was also an outstanding success in terms of business: at the negotiations in Bombay he managed to secure an order worth a large amount of money for the factory he represented.

Even the foreign press showed a keen interest in his honeymoon; it caused quite a stir that the Hungarian head of state was so confident in the safety of flying that he allowed his son to take his young wife on a flying honeymoon.

Vitéz István Horthy's flying feats were not only very significant as sporting achievements, but also provided invaluable propaganda for civilian air transport. The public heard and read that the son of the country's leader had arrived in London at the time previously arranged, despite the weather conditions; that later, as deputy managing director of the country's most important factory, he had flown on urgent business from Budapest to Bombay and back in a small private plane; and that he had set off with his young wife on a 15 day honeymoon in a plane with just a 100 horse power engine, without a radio or a radio operator to pick up weather forecasts en route, without a co-pilot to take over if he got tired, and without a mechanic who knew every nut and bolt in the engine and could provide help at once if necessary: in contrast, the public enjoyed all these safety measures, and flew in planes with two or three engines of 800-1000 horse power each. Vitéz István Horthy's flying achievements did more to promote air transport than ten years of favourable accident statistics.

(The author, Vitéz Rezső Laborczffy, is president of the board of MALÉRT [*Magyar Légiforgalmi Részvénytársaság—Hungarian Air Transport Company*].

The text is taken from "Vitéz Nagybányai Horthy István élete és a magyar közlekedés". [*The Life of Vitéz István Horthy de Nagybánya and Transport in Hungary*], edited by Olaf Wulff and Jenő Maleter; Budapest 1943, pp. 245–248.)

Sándor Ember:
A FEW BRUSHSTROKES OF A PORTRAIT OF ISTVÁN HORTHY AS A PILOT
(Extracts)

...István Horthy was a genuine technical specialist. He worked purposefully to acquire, down to the smallest details, the necessary technical knowledge he needed to perform his duties in the best possible way. He strove to keep abreast of the latest developments in all areas of technology, to the extent that he could make an accurate assessment of their significance and fit them into the right place in his mental picture of the relationship between man and technology. He was not one of those romantics who immediately attribute earth-shattering significance to every technical innovation sparked off by invention. But István Horthy was a born creator: in addition to his practical common sense, he certainly had the necessary powers of imagination. Thus he could paint a picture of the future with persuasive conviction and show correctly the direction progress was taking. ...

...He always carried his slide rule in his pocket, and often tried to obtain an exact mathematical solution to problems in cases where others would have been satisfied with less precise methods. However, despite being technically very highly educated, he was by no means a narrow specialist. His broad general education, his extraordinary intuitive ability, and his sound sense of proportion gave him a wide perspective over problems and enabled him to rationalise them. His real ambition was to acquire all the theoretical knowledge and practical experience required to carry out as effectively as possible the duties he had undertaken in his profession of engineering. The fact that he achieved this aim gave him a conscious and superior confidence which no unforeseen situation could shake. The knowledge that he was a true expert in the profession he had chosen, and that his expertise gave him control over a significant sector of his life, together with his intuitive mentality, made him so confident in the application of knowledge he had acquired in other areas that he was able to be versatile without being superficial. ...

...In this paper I cannot paint anything like a complete picture of all the work he did to promote every branch of aviation in Hungary. The lasting things he created are a memorial to him. It would take an exhaustive analysis filling an entire volume just to recount the work he put into the training of young Hungarian pilots, and into the organisation and implementation of pilot training outside the armed forces. What he did to develop the aircraft industry, specialist training for the aircraft industry, and aircraft design, and how he strengthened the air force and air transport could also form the subject of a separate analysis. ...

...How did István Horthy become a pilot?

In the mid-1920s, when the handful of men constituting the Hungarian air force—operating under heavy disguise, in civilian clothes and with contrived titles, though with full military and air force discipline—could at last begin to think in terms of training reservists to provide the next generation of pilots, István Horthy was one of the first to volunteer. He considered his voluntary service as proper professional training. The life of these volunteer pilots was very different from the good life enjoyed by pilots in the peaceful times before the first world war. Those who wanted to be officers in the air force had to have a broad and detailed knowledge of the science of flying.

Practical pilot training requires the utmost attention

and discipline. They started early, getting into their planes at first light and completing tasks which required unfailing concentration, the utmost alertness, presence of mind, determination, and a strong, well-focused will to succeed. By the time they had completed their military training on the ground, their theoretical studies, and maintenance work on their planes, they would fall into bed exhausted. Of course, staying up late and parties going on into the small hours were out of the question, because this would have been very detrimental to the high level of physical fitness which pilot training required. Saturday was the only day on which the camp's strict discipline allowed them to stay up longer together, with the natural exception of those who were on duty. But in order to be fresh for the dawn flight on Monday, the volunteers had to go to bed on Sunday night as early as schoolchildren in a dormitory. These first volunteers were even denied the pleasure of promenading in uniform, because Hungary was forbidden to have an air force, and anyone who dedicated himself to that could not advertise the fact.

Usually the men who volunteered to serve as pilots were the ones who were attracted by flying, and so were prepared to endure all the discomfort, tiredness, and constraints which pilot training imposed on its novices to a far greater extent than training for the other services. István Horthy's superior officers who taught him to fly were among the best pilots who had served in the first world war, and their relationship with the young pilots was strict, demanding disciplined behaviour, but also understanding and fraternal. Any of the novices who were not suited to life as pilots were soon weeded out, but then the rest became a much more close-knit family, officers and men, novices and old hands together. In this community of colleagues, both during his initial training and later, when he joined the fighter squadron, István

Horthy was the perfect example of a serious, well-trained air force officer, a colleague, and a genial gentleman, and remained so until his heroic death in a flying accident. He is remembered as such in the many writings which have appeared and the many true stories currently circulating about him. A particular characteristic of István Horthy both during his initial training and during his subsequent military service, when he took part in exercises and—from 1938 onwards—in the various mobilisations of the national defence forces, was that beyond performing the duties assigned to him in any posting, he observed, studied and examined in minute detail the planes and other technical equipment, the organisation, the location, the airfields, the training, the exercises, and every aspect of the service in general. He joined in the camaraderie of military life in an informal manner, just like any other officer. But sharp-eyed observers were able to see that while his behaviour conformed in every respect to his subordinate position in the service, he still observed everything from above. He noticed both what was good and as it should be, and what was deficient, what was outdated, and what had to be and could be improved. His critical eye saw the smallest details, but only a brief remark would indicate that he had already made a correct assessment of the improvements that could be made and how even more could be achieved. But it was later, when he was together with those colleagues who fought alongside him for the cause of aviation in Hungary, and when, representing the flying institutions he led, he had to stand up for the cause before the competent authorities, that his thorough grounding, his sharp powers of judgement, his far-seeing conception, and his practical common sense which never missed realistic opportunities, really became apparent. His observations were comprehensive: he did not get bogged down in details but always focused sharply on the essentials, and having made a criticism, he would also immediately point out the solution which was right, expedient, and attainable.

More than fifteen years passed until that fateful St Stephen's day on which he died a heroic death, and during those years István Horthy worked with determination for the cause of aviation in Hungary, giving the best of his talent in order to play his part in making it great.

The desire to get to know the sea and distant worlds which had led his father as a young boy to join the navy was also present in István Horthy. In 1918, when we lost Fiume, István Horthy had to leave the naval academy. After that it was flying and the oceans of the air which replaced for him the navy and the vast empire of the seas. István Horthy longed to get to know the world: he could never resign himself to his country being landlocked, and though he never gave up the hope that one day we would have access to the sea again, he said that Hungarians must at all costs break out of their isolation through the ocean of the air. He said we must not resign ourselves to our reduced circumstances, we must not submit helplessly to our fate and to the whims of other countries.

It is stimulating for Hungarians to get to know the lives of those nations which are at the forefront of culture, and to learn from them what is good and what can be put into practice here. On the other hand, it increases our self-confidence if other nations get to know us and learn to appreciate our culture. He thought that the further we can extend the links—both economic and intellectual—which we build with other continents, the more significant the role we can play in international life, and the more the aspirations of the Hungarian people will be attained. He was rooted by his sentiments and his origins in Hungarian soil, but his far-seeing eyes looked far beyond Hungary's constrained borders.

István Horthy also considered it a dangerous problem

that only a very small number of young Hungarians were able to train as sailors. In the foreseeable future those Hungarians who grew to manhood in the navy will be gone, and there are insufficient replacements. The spiritual composition of a cultured people—he thought—must not lack the sailors' typical character, outlook on life, and experience of having seen the world. However, at the moment it is so difficult for enough young Hungarians to join the navy that these sailors' characteristics will no longer be noticeable in our national character. As well as being very important in its own right, flying has the significance that its character-building strength is similar in many respects to that of the navy. It enriches the character with new features. We can obtain a fleet of aircraft with our own resources even in our landlocked isolation. We can break out of the constriction placed on us by Trianon through the ocean of the air, and if we link in to the developing world-wide network of passenger flights with our own far-reaching routes, we will not only gain immeasurable economic benefits, but also win high esteem for Hungary in the area of aviation. And we will also bring those Hungarians living abroad closer to home—István Horthy was also concerned with the fate of Hungarians living abroad.

Talking to his friends, he often said how much it hurt him to hear the Hungarians who had emigrated to America saying that they longed to visit the old country, but it was so hard to get there. They would have to travel on foreign ships and through foreign countries, and most of them were very reluctant to undertake such an adventurous journey through a Europe torn apart after the war, where they needed so many transit permits and visas and had to cross areas speaking so many languages to get to the old country. The Germans, the Italians, the Spaniards and the other maritime nations could maintain permanent links between a large proportion of their emigres and the home country using their own ships. Our Hungarians abroad could not experience a similar comforting link whereby the ship which went across the sea to fetch them was a Hungarian one, and once aboard the ship in a foreign port they were already on Hungarian territory. This is what they missed and regretted, and this is what made many ordinary people finally sever their links with the old country. He said he saw what a festive occasion it was for people of other nationalities living in America when they saw their own country's ship enter an American port flying their own flag. How well this kept alive in them the feeling of belonging to their native land! Only the Hungarians in America could not share in this uplifting sentiment, because it was very rarely that one of the half dozen low-tonnage Hungarian merchant ships which plied the oceans of the world went to those American ports where large numbers of Hungarians lived; and there were no passenger ships on the seas at all which flew the Hungarian flag. If a Hungarian company transporting passengers by air managed to link in to international air transport in such a way that Hungarian pilots could fly in planes with Hungarian markings on intercontinental routes, what a broad perspective this would open to Hungarian passenger flights! And how it would raise the self-assurance of Hungarians abroad, particularly those in America, if Hungarian passenger planes could reach the American continent. ...

...The final summary was always the same: we must do our utmost to lay the foundations by developing and bringing up to date the Hungarian aircraft industry, the training of aircraft workers and engineers, the design of aircraft, and the theoretical and practical study of flying, and by providing experimental stations. But we had to start immediately to organise initial pilot training for young people in as many places as possible, by developing a framework over the whole country for modelling, gliding, training in powered flight outside the armed forces, and then keeping these young pilots in training. The development of Hungarian air transport in the most up-to-date manner was another issue which could not wait. Beoming involved in international air transport as far as possible, building suitable airports, acquiring airliners and flying them on internal routes covering the whole country and the on widest possible network of international routes: all these would not only strengthen the organisation of transport, but also serve the interests of national defence. ...

...István Horthy often had exhaustive discussions with the most outstanding Hungarian pilots about the development of Hungarian air transport. These discussions convinced him that MALÉRT [*Magyar Légiforgalmi Részvénytársaság—Hungarian Air Transport Company*] had to be made not just formally but institutionally as independent as possible. The more successfully this company achieves its primary aim of flying as many kilometres as possible on internal and international routes, transporting as many passengers and as much freight and mail as possible, the better this will serve its longer-term aims of keeping many outstanding pilots in training and of increasing the numbers of flying technical staff and ground-based service staff, all of whom could in the event of war be transferred at a moment's notice, even within the framework of MALÉRT, to national defence service.

By the spring of 1938 we had progressed beyond the planning stage in the question of training young people to fly. We had taken in hand the reorganisation and the direction of the Hungarian Aero Society, and were making further plans. István Horthy always said that Hungarian aviation could only be developed to perfection within a unified organisation, as the example of other countries has shown. One of the most important branches of this unified organisation is air transport. Hungarian airline pilots have a good reputation outside as well as within the country. So if they are given modern and good airliners, if MALÉRT is able to equip itself appropriately, now that traffic between continents and across oceans is increasing rapidly with the building of long-range aircraft, then it too could get intercontinental routes. ...

... Some official quarters were actually very disconcerted by István Horthy's vigour, since the requirements he set up when expressed in financial terms came to previously unimagined totals. But he explained that our aviation organisation had to be equipped immediately with planes from abroad, so that by the time our aircraft industry reached the required capacity and was able to deliver planes from the production line, the pilots would already be competent in their duties. This was the only way we could ensure the effectiveness of our air force and achieve the success we wanted for MALÉRT in the international air transport network.

István Horthy immediately set about equipping MÁVAG to manufacture 100 horse power Hirth engines for small training and practice planes, and would have liked MÁVAG and the other factories and secondary industries associated with aircraft manufacture to develop their works as quickly as possible for this task.

This considerable activity by István Horthy aroused great hopes in the flying community in Hungary and put an end to their pessimism. Everyone hoped on the one hand that István Horthy would help to achieve vital organisational changes which would ensure that suitably qualified experts would be in charge of aviation at the highest level, and on the other hand that we could start working at full strength to recover the ground we had lost. ...

...1939 started as the year in which aviation in Hungary was reborn, and the main credit for this is due to

István Horthy. He had already worked very hard before then: he considered that any worthwhile man should do at least eight hours of useful work every day. He arranged his working hours at MÁVAG on this basis; then he gained a large amount of additional work associated with his presidency of the Hungarian Aero Society and then the Horthy Miklós National Flying Foundation. This was primarily organisational and building work of a type which could not be restricted to schedules or time limits. In addition, he regularly worked on problems relating to other areas of aviation, primarily the aircraft industry, the training of aircraft engineers, and air transport, but also problems relating to the air force. It was an extensive and complex collection of tasks which would not fit any set pattern, requiring new deliberations each day as well as a knowledge of aviation in the countries he had chosen as examples. The only way he could tackle this was by working so solidly that apart from a quick lunch in the MÁVAG canteen he had no more than a cup of tea before getting back to the palace around midnight after the last aviation meeting of the day. Yet he did not show any signs of tiredness, partly because he could stand the pace, and partly because he never lost his self-control and could always keep himself alert. The example of István Horthy also inspired almost every member of the family of pilots in Hungary to do their utmost. This produced immediate results, which naturally made them redouble their efforts.

In the meantime István Horthy made two flights abroad in small private planes and in unusual and unfavourable weather conditions. These gave aviation experts proof of his practical flying ability, his skill in navigation, his courage, and the particular qualities which made him eminently suited to being a pilot; and gained him the utmost respect abroad as well.

In May 1939, flying his small Becker training plane

alone all the way, he crossed a continent chilled by cumulus clouds and furrowed by storms to reach London. Of six similar planes taking off in Budapest his was the only one to arrive. Our pilots, led by István Horthy as president of the Hungarian Aero Society, were due to return the visits of English pilots who had participated in the pilots' picnics held in Hungary in the preceding years. In the weather conditions prevailing at the time, it seemed unlikely that the simple mass-produced training planes, which were not equipped with radios or instruments for flying in fog, would be able to arrive in London at the appointed time. Pilots with outstanding practical experience were forced by the cloud and the storms to disperse soon after taking off; some returned, while others spent days kicking their heels at intermediate airports. Only István Horthy arrived punctually at the intermediate airports, and then in London. Of course many people said: "Yes, of course he can fly, but it was by chance and good fortune that he could make the journey so punctually in such bad weather." A few weeks later I talked to some English pilots in London—I had been unable to take part in the visit planned for May because of the parliamentary election, and only travelled there by passenger plane at the beginning of June. Their opinion was different, particularly as they had examined István Horthy's small training plane closely on his arrival. They acknowledged that it was a real feat of aviation for him to have arrived at the appointed hour having flown through so many areas of storm and cloud—the weather over Britain in May is usually very unsettled. This shows not only that István Horthy is a polite man who does not want to waste the time of those who are expecting him, but also that he is a very skilled navigator.

In early June 1939 István Horthy travelled to London again, this time on a passenger plane. He was there on important business for MÁVAG, and apart from the day of the Derby at Ascot, the main event of the season - and of course weekends, when it is very difficult to get anyone in England to carry on his trade—István Horthy worked all day. For the Derby the Duke of Kent invited him to his box. When we occasionally got together for an hour at mealtimes, we agreed that in London there was an unmistakable general atmosphere of preparation for war. But somehow we still could not believe that war could be so close, since common sense dictated that the enormous risk involved in a three-dimensional war, where the large-scale deployment of aeroplanes had terrible potential for destruction, could still be averted at the negotiating table with a little goodwill. István Horthy half-jokingly remarked that if they really were preparing for war, then the presumptive opponents should at least wait until MÁVAG completed its business. This was necessary to enable MÁVAG to put its finances in order and carry out its factory development programme. That was when he mentioned that he wanted to obtain orders and work for MÁVAG from India, and he said that if it proved necessary for him to travel there, though this was the wrong season from the point of view of weather conditions, he would try with the small Aradó 79 to get to Bombay in time. The point was that he had to return to Budapest to prepare for the negotiations in India, and if he had to travel on a scheduled passenger flight, he would not be able to get from Budapest to Bombay in time. It was also by no means certain that he would be able to get a seat on the passenger plane. When he saw that I was taken aback by his plan, he did not mention it again; nor did he speak about it in Budapest on his return. I only found out by chance on 17th June that he had secretly made preparations for his journey to India and had reached the stage where he intended to set off for Bombay the next day in the small Aradó plane, alone, without any escort. I immediately told Vitéz László Háry, the then commander of the air force, who shared my anxiety to such an extent that he reported the matter at once to the Regent, who was in Gödöllő at the time, unaware that his son wanted to set off alone in a small private plane on this long and difficult journey. However, István Horthy's arguments prevailed, the Regent gave his permission, and István Horthy, as is well known, flew some 13,000 km to Bombay and back, completing his journey, as with the flight to London, as regularly as clockwork.

With this flight he proved what he had always said, that a private plane is as valuable as any other form of transport if its pilot understands its function properly, knows how to handle it, and can navigate. It can overcome distance and time as no form of land transport can.

Thus we watched as István Horthy grew to become the leader of Hungarian aviation on the basis of his abilities, his work, his successes and his achievements as a pilot. The old campaigners of aviation, who had been through many hardships and disappointments but had never lost hope, lined up behind their leader, together with the young generation.

In 1940 we were delighted to hear of István Horthy's engagement to Countess Ilona Edelsheim-Gyulai. He soon took his fiancée to Budaörs airport and made several flights with her in his Aradó private plane. After each trip he would happily tell me that his fiancée was very talented, and that he had immediately started teaching her to fly with the dual controls in the passenger seat, with such success that he was happy to let her fly the plane while airborne.

After their wedding at the end of April 1940, they naturally set off on their honeymoon in the small plane. First they flew to Italy, then they crossed the Mediterranean via Sicily to Africa. In Benghazi they were the guests of the legendary Italian pilot Italo Balbo, who as governor of Libya had his residence there. In Egypt the young couple were the guests of King Farouk, who was also a pilot, and was just then awaiting the arrival of two M 24 private planes he had ordered from the Budapest Technical University's Amateur Flying Club.

His honeymoon journey in the small private plane which he and his wife, the most charming novice pilot, took turns to fly and maintained together, was another demonstration of how well the private plane could be used as a form of transport.

The first peak in the impetus given to aviation in Hungary by István Horthy occurred in 1940. We all thought that once the recovery had started, development would continue at the same pace. We hoped that with István Horthy's leadership an Air Ministry would be formed in which he would unify all aviation bodies with unlimited powers. Unfortunately the frost once again froze the tree of our hope just when it was in full flower. A man of his calibre was also needed to lead MÁV, and those who had charge of the country's affairs decided that aviation could wait a little longer for his full-time work, and took him away from us to be president of MÁV, to duties which were undeniably extremely important, but also extremely difficult.

However, even as president of the State Railways he did not loosen his links with aviation. He did resign as president of the Hungarian Aero Society, but he stayed on as president of the Horthy Miklós National Flying Foundation, and within a couple of weeks of his arrival the office of the president of the State Railways already looked like the intellectual centre of Hungarian aviation affairs. This continued until his election as Vice-Regent.

When the parliament elected him Vice-Regent, we felt that we had won him for the cause of aviation, with all his capacity for work and with increased powers. After all, the Regent had placed him in charge of aviation in Hungary immediately after his election. István Horthy's infinite modesty was the only reason why he did not immediately take matters into his hands as the pilots' "field-marshal" but first went out to the front as Flight Lt. Vitéz Horthy to gain experience of the war and to show an example of military and flying virtues. In May 1942 I visited him at Szolnok with Count Gyula Károlyi. My secret aim was to try to dissuade him, the man destined to lead the country, from risking his life at the head of a small unit, as a squad leader in a flying squadron, when the whole country was expecting so much of him. This attempt was futile. He replied that when he came back in September, then with his experience of war he would be better able to do everything we expected of him in aviation. He said that he was concerned about the future of MALÉRT, and now that he is no longer alive, it is as if the words he spoke at our last meeting were his last will and testament. He concluded that MALÉRT must continue to develop despite the war, that its fleet of planes must not be reduced, on the contrary it must be greatly increased and MALÉRT's organisation must be improved, developed and strengthened. The company's independence must be maintained and defended. Apart from the fact that MALÉRT is performing the difficult task of transporting men and materials between Hungary and the front, we must make sure that it wins as many scheduled international routes as possible, over the longest possible range, at least between the countries which are friendly to us, as this will prepare it for the tasks to come after the war.

We awaited his return impatiently: we missed him greatly in dealing with the tasks—primarily relating to aviation—which the Regent had given him. Then the terrible news arrived: István Horthy had sacrificed his life for his country and for the cause of aviation.

His life was that of a fulfilled man. His family lives on in István, the young son he leaves behind. His work has already produced lasting results. He contributed farsighted plans and bold ideas to the work of laying the foundations of aviation in Hungary. His manly, hardworking life, the courageous way in which he stood up for his convictions, his persistent endurance in the struggle, his willpower, his discipline, his loyalty to his colleagues, his achievements as a pilot, his military behaviour, and the sacrifice of his life for his country make him a lasting example to us all. If our heart's desire is to make Hungarian aviation great, let us endeavour to advance along the path which István Horthy has marked out!

(The author, Dr. Sándor Ember, is a deputy in the Hungarian Parliament and president of the Horthy Miklós National Flying Foundation.

The text is taken from "Vitéz Nagybányai Horthy István élete és a magyar közlekedés" [*The Life of Vitéz István Horthy de Nagybánya and Transport in Hungary*], edited by Olaf Wulff and Jenő Maleter; Budapest 1943, pp. 221–241.)

György ("Gyuri") Farkas:
MY MASTER—AS I SAW HIM

AT MÁVAG

When I became István Horthy's valet, he was deputy managing director of MÁVAG [*Magyar Állami Vas-, Acél- és Gépgyár—Hungarian Iron, Steel and Engineering Works*]. Many people have written about his work there: the press at the time, and after his death the managing director himself, Jenő Markotay-Velsz, and many others who had official contacts with him and wrote about their memories of him. These memoirs were also published as a book in Hungary, and then in Canada after the war. But copies of the book were sold so quickly that I couldn't get hold of one when I was in Toronto. I thought if I couldn't buy a copy, at least I would borrow one from someone so that I could read it. I asked everyone I knew, but without success. Finally, back at home, Providence granted my wish. I received a copy from the best-qualified person, István Horthy's widow. I was very pleased that those whose writings appeared in the book had written the truth, based on direct, living, personal contacts with him, without hearsay, without any outside control, and without any ill-will. I'm glad they wrote about him, because in this way the nation could obtain true information about the life of the Vice-Regent after his heroic death.

Now I would like to remember as well. I want to write about the ordinary days, the everyday life of the factory workers and the former deputy managing director: the office, the workplace, the personal, human contacts.

The working day started at 8 o'clock in the morning,

but it was the done thing to arrive at work before eight. Even the boss went to work in his own transport. István Horthy had seen this in America, where he worked in the Ford factory, and he adhered to it with MÁVAG. MÁVAG did have an official car, but Lelovics, the driver, only went to pick up the deputy managing director if he was starting work early in the morning not in the factory but in some other official place, with early negotiations in the ministry or elsewhere, and then going on to the factory. The car was available for him during the day too, but if he had any private business, he always went in his own car. He didn't even use the factory's car if, for instance, after an afternoon meeting which went on late he didn't go back to the factory. He never used the factory's car on Saturday afternoons, Sundays, or holidays, even if he had official business: a works sporting or other event.

István Horthy never kept anyone waiting, but he also expected his colleagues to be punctual to the minute. If on a rare occasion someone did arrive a few minutes late, the deputy managing director would very politely invite him to take a seat. But there was something in this polite welcome which made the person wish he hadn't been late and resolve that he would never be late again.

The deputy managing director used the gate at no.1 Kőbányai Street. Mr Berta, the gatekeeper, opened the big iron gate between five and eight minutes before eight o'clock, but István Horthy was always first with his greeting. Mr Berta was a strange-looking, plump man, well into his fifties. He wore blue overalls which had faded in many washes, or a coat, with a tatty cloth cap on his head. He whipped this off quickly when greeting my master, and then his bald head shone out like moonlight. It looked strange over his sun-tanned face. I often accompanied my master to the factory and sensed that somehow this was bothering him. Perhaps he smiled inwardly, but I could tell that he wouldn't tolerate it for long. Then one day he asked:

"Mr Berta, aren't you supposed to get a service uniform?"

"I did have one, Your Highness, but I haven't been given one for years, though I'm an employee of MÁV. This whole factory belongs to MÁV, and me with it."

One or two weeks passed, and the cloth cap was still in service. Once, when we got up to the office, Jenő Oszkár Hille, his secretary, was waiting, and as he returned my master's 'good morning,' my master said to him:

"Oszkár, I have given instructions that Mr Berta should be given his uniform allowance. Please see to it that Mr Berta reports to me tomorrow in uniform. He should just salute instead of snatching that cloth cap off his head. He's supposed to have a uniform anyway, he just hasn't been given one yet for some reason."

I should add that Mr Berta got a special reward from István Horthy every Christmas for opening the gate each day. On one occasion, after the usual Christmas Eve celebrations in the palace, when the Regent and his wife had given the family's staff their presents by the Christmas tree, István Horthy remembered that he hadn't given Mr Berta his reward. He told me to put 100 pengős in an envelope, drive over to Mr Berta's with it straight away, and wish him a merry Christmas on his behalf. The good man got almost a month's pay in the envelope.

MÁV had a works canteen where everyone who worked there could eat very cheaply. Anyone from the managing director to temporary workers could use the canteen. The only difference was that the managers' tables had tablecloths while the workers' tables didn't. Everyone took this for granted, after all in a half hour lunch break they couldn't take off their oily, grimy clothes, have a shower, and put on clean clothes to sit down at the table. That was the way things had to be.

Everyone had a free choice of food. István Horthy regularly ate there with the workers, most of whom he knew by name, even though they had no idea that he did. They were surprised when he called them by name. He even used the factory's barber, who also went to his home to cut his hair later on, when he was president of MÁV. In short, he had very close contacts with the factory workers. Even I was surprised, as I listened to a radio programme which was part of May Day celebrations sometime in the seventies, to hear two workers speaking about his direct contacts with his fellow workers.

I have already mentioned the Ford factory in America where István Horthy, newly-qualified as an engineer, was employed as a worker. In the various places he worked, he strove to learn the most highly developed forms of the production methods of the time—and I should add that he was most diligent and successful in this. Then, back at home, he did his best to use in MÁVAG the methods he had seen.

By 1936–1937 the capital's fleet of taxis was very antiquated. The Magomobiles with their wooden wheels were causing severe problems for the grey and blue taxi companies. Then MÁVAG began mass-producing a Ford car, making use of a well-trained team of engineers and good connections with Ford. Unfortunately the war prevented further development, but even so the taxi companies ran a good number of these new Hungarian cars around Budapest.

The threat of war then made it necessary to promote aviation, train pilots, and possibly develop a Hungarian plane. MÁVAG started test manufacture. An aircraft assembly workshop was built on the corner of Kőbányai Street and Örs Vezér Square. One of István Horthy's most enthusiastic associates was the chief engineer, Takács, a young engineer about the same age as him. They worked very enthusiastically and successfully. The fact that pilots could be trained at all in Hungary at that time, the foundation of the National Flying Foundation and the Aero Society, the rapid increase in the numbers of glider and powered aircraft pilots: all these were due mainly to the work of István Horthy and his colleagues. A close-knit and skilled team worked together with István Horthy, who was the kind of leader who wasn't afraid to pick up the tools himself when necessary. And we should remember that nobody was entitled to more pay for this extra work. Everyone was paid according to his government post.

István Horthy lived off his salary. It's true that he didn't have accommodation expenses: he lived with his parents in the Castle, where he had an "apartment" consisting of just one room, which had its own bathroom. It was furnished with just the essentials, without any luxuries. He repaid every last filler of the loan he received from his parents to buy a car. His financial situation improved when his uncle István Horthy, a retired cavalry general, died. The uncle was also my master's godfather. His wife, Margit Latinovits, had died at the end of the 1920s, and they had no children. The Latinovits family had at one time been very rich; now all that remained of their fortune was an estate of 1100 cadastral holds [*627 hectares*] at Katymár. After his uncle's death in 1937, the younger István Horthy, his godson, inherited the estate and the newly-built family house. That was when his financial situation began to improve. The estate was rented by a co-operative of about 20 farmers in Katymár. However, this extra income was held in a completely separate account. My master carried on living off his salary, though this was before the time when managers were given bonuses amounting to several times their annual salary. Every state employee—regardless of their post—received a month's salary at the end of the year, and half a month's salary at Easter. This went for the managing director and the servant alike. I have just recorded all this here so that we can have some idea of István Horthy's income.

On the basis of his achievements in developing transport, which were recognised both by the government of the time and by leading experts, it was almost a foregone conclusion that István Horthy would be appointed head of the State Railways to succeed the retiring president Kornél Láner.

TO INDIA IN A PRIVATE PLANE

If I remember rightly, I once read in a newspaper article that István Horthy flew in his own plane to Bombay in India in order to make himself popular. How naive! If the journalist doesn't know the subject, why does he write about it? And most of all, why does he write things which are not true, thus deceiving the reader? Well, of course, not so long ago in a certain kind of paper the author of such writings could publish them without any problem—in fact he could gain credit for them. On the other hand, if he had written the truth, he would hardly have been praised for it—if indeed he had been allowed to publish it at all.

Well, the truth is that even István Horthy's father, the Regent of Hungary, found out about this plane journey at the last moment, and not from his son—who had made preparations for the flight in the utmost secrecy—but from the commander of the air force, who, having found out about it, felt it was his duty to report the matter to the Regent, who was away from Budapest at the time.

Although my master prepared for the journey in secret, I still had to know about it, since I took part in the rapid preparations. And of course J. Oszkár Hille, who was head of deputy managing director István Horthy's secretariat at MÁVAG, must have known about it too. But apart from this, the important journey was surrounded by the deepest secrecy even within MÁVAG.

So what really happened, and why was the journey so important? The year was 1939; it was summer, the end of June, if I remember rightly. The second world war hadn't broken out yet, but there was definitely gunpowder in the air. It was hot. There were just the two of us in the palace, because the Regent and his family usually spent the summer months in Gödöllő or Kenderes. Then my master István Horthy said to me:

"Tomorrow I'm going to Munich on the morning flight. Pack the essential things in my small flying bag. If everything goes well, I'll be back in the afternoon. I'll bring the plane, or if not my plane, then another one on loan."

I knew that in 1938 he had ordered an Aradó 79 plane for himself, but the Germans—perhaps because of the events leading up to the war—weren't able to deliver it by the agreed date. They didn't change the contract or the delivery date, they just didn't deliver it. After telephone discussions they finally offered a plane on loan.

This Aradó 79 was a very attractive plane. The two seats were side by side, and the luggage space was behind the seats. Anyone who knows the planes of that period will know it was not just a nice looking aircraft but also fast and reliable. But it's not the plane I want to talk about now.

My further orders were that while he was away, I was to go to the Foreign Ministry to see Miss Irma Kern. I was to take his diplomatic passport with me and have it prepared for him to travel to India. Through the military office I was to get hold of maps from the Army Cartographic Institue. I was not to breathe a word about what we wanted them for. I knew someone in the military office personally, and if I asked him for something for my master, he could arrange it without any questions being asked.

The next morning we went out to Budaörs, which was where the civil airport was then. My master left, and I got on with the arrangements. I also bought the necessary pounds from the Fő utca branch of the English-Hungarian Bank, where we had a current account. This didn't attract any attention, since I was the one who dealt with the bank and with the books of the household accounts. But at that time I still didn't know what all this was needed for. By the time I'd got everything done it was quite late, time for me to go back to the airport to await his arrival. He got back in the early evening. After we had duly admired the plane, we put it in MÁVAG's hangar and then went home.

That was when the hard work started. My master asked me whether there was anything to eat, as he hadn't eaten anything since morning. There was a bit of butter, cheese, and sausage which I'd got for breakfast. In summer no cooked meals were provided in the palace. István Horthy usually had lunch in the factory, even when meals were provided at home. The family usually got together for supper, and then I ate there too, naturally with the staff. In the summer months I ate with the guards. But today I was hungry too, I hadn't had time even to snatch a quick lunch. As we were both feeling the effects of a missed lunch, my master told me to put the maps, compass, and other drawing instruments on the big table in the Mátyás room, and arrange for a substantial supper.

I set everything out while he had a bath to relax after his tiring day. I rang the restaurant opposite the Horváth Gardens, where the speciality and the owner's recommendation was székelykáposzta [*a dish consisting of a mixture of meat, braised with onions and paprika, and sauerkraut*]. I ordered two large portions and asked for them to be put on a tray for me to collect, but I wanted a waiter to come as well to serve it here, and I'd take him back afterwards. Another phone call: I ordered sandwiches for my master to eat on the plane, and a thermos flask of fresh ice-cold water. I made him a litre of tea in another thermos flask before he left.

So we had a good supper, and plenty of it, and my master's enthusiasm for work returned. I took the waiter back, collected the sandwiches, and started packing. My master plotted the route on his maps. It was midnight by the time we got to bed. I asked the guards to wake us at four o'clock in the morning. By five we were in the hangar at Budaörs. I helped start the plane, and soon István Horthy took off for Bombay. He told me about his intermediate stops afterwards. All he said before he left was:

"You will be informed of my arrival. If my mother asks where I am, just tell her I've gone abroad."

Now I knew where he was going, but I still didn't know why he had to set off on this long journey in such a hurry.

A day or two later the director of MALÉRT, whom I knew personally, phoned and asked me to take my master's dress suit and everything else he needed to the office in a bag, and they would pack it up and send it off to India. The viceroy was giving a reception in honour of István Horthy, that was why he needed the dress suit. I knew what protocol required for such occasions. As well as the dress suit I packed his decorations, the three shirt buttons consisting of emeralds set in platinum, the matching cufflinks, and also his gold pocket watch with platinum chain. Naturally I got out his new dress suit.

Well, to cut a long story short, the dress suit never got there; my master found some other way to dress for the reception. We got the package back from MALÉRT eight months later, unopened and intact. As the director said, it had even been transported by camel. We had it cleaned, and it continued to be the new dress suit.

The Regent found out the details of his son's journey to Bombay from foreign reports, but by that time the aim of the journey had been achieved: the contract had been signed. He got home safely. The Regent met his son at

Budaörs airport. Of course the general public still didn't know the real reason for this arduous journey. Its novelty value was blurred by other events: the war was starting, the papers had enough to write about. However, it was certainly a bold undertaking. It's not comfortable or even safe to travel between the sky and the ground in the hot sun, to sleep under the plane on airfields, and to land in the tropical heat of Bombay, with the temperature at 52 °C. Not many people would undertake such a journey even in today's modern planes with all their safety equipment.

So why did he go? Very few people knew that even after he had returned home, apart from his closest colleagues. It is a fact that making himself popular was not his aim.

In 1939 India invited bids for the delivery of one hundred 424 type express steam locomotives. There were two companies in Hungary which manufactured locomotives: one was MÁVAG, which was owned by MÁV, and the other was Ganz és Társa Villamossági, Gép- Waggon és Hajógyár Részvénytársaság [*Ganz & Co. Electrical, Machine, Wagon and Shipbuilding Company*], known as GANZ. The two giant factories were neighbours—both had works on the Kőbányai Street—and both manufactured the world-famous 424s. An order from abroad for one hundred such locomotives was a deal of enormous significance. Naturally it was those high-level managers who were authorised to sign the contract who had to travel to the negotiations. In order to secure an advantage in the business negotiations, GANZ had bought up the available seats on the flight to Bombay well in advance. It's important to know that at that time there was only one flight per week between London and Bombay, and generally only one or two seats could be reserved in Budapest. Naturally when the plane landed in Budapest it could only take those passengers with reservations, so despite all his prestige and good personal connections, István Horthy couldn't get a ticket for the passenger flight. This annoyed him immensely. He could see that he couldn't travel to the negotiations as a competitor on equal terms. In addition it mattered to him whether it was the Hungarian company he led which could deliver the hundred locomotives, or GANZ, which was a partly German concern. He knew that if he couldn't travel there now—and his business competitors had done everything to prevent him from doing so—then the deal would certainly be lost.

It was these reasons which induced him to undertake the perilous journey alone in a private plane. Of course it was also annoying that the German firm, referring to the war situation, didn't deliver the Aradó 79 he had ordered by the agreed date. However, he managed to overcome this difficulty through lengthy phone calls, as a result of which the German factory—as I mentioned before—was prepared to loan him a plane for one flight there and back, for the duration of the negotiations.

By the time GANZ's delegation arrived in Bombay on the scheduled flight, the contract had already been signed with MÁVAG. This is the genuine and true story of the flight to Bombay: there was never any question of making himself popular, though it's undeniable that the outstanding achievement popularised the sportsman. But that happens nowadays too.

AT THE HEAD OF THE STATE RAILWAYS

1940 saw a significant change in István Horthy's life: first of all his marriage—changed circumstances, a new apartment to furnish instead of the single room he'd had before. His mother and his wife took charge of that with a great deal of loving care. They moved into a four-room apartment on the second floor of the royal palace, on the south side of the Krisztina Boulevard wing.

The second change was that immediately after his marriage he was appointed president of MÁV. I should add that in the autumn of that year the return of parts of Transylvania to Hungary led to a significant increase in the area of the country.

Kornél Láner, the previous president of MÁV, was retiring, and István Horthy was his successor. Others who are experts on the subject have written about the kind of transport specialist he was and what he did for the development of rail transport as well as transport in Hungary generally. I would just like to describe a few incidents which actually happened.

In 1940 a high-level delegation took part in negotiations between Hungary and Romania in Kolozsvár. The negotiations were led by Pál Álgyay-Hubert, a state secretary representing the ministry, and István Horthy, the president of the board representing MÁV. When the talks had been completed, we spent another two or three days in Transylvania and the leaders drove around a large part of the road network in order to find out what needed to be done. The public roads in Transylvania were in a very bad state. In one place we could only struggle slowly along the bumpy, neglected, narrow road. On either side of the road there were closely spaced small mounds overgrown with weeds, stretching over several kilometres. The state secretary and the president were intrigued as to what these mounds at the roadside could be. It turned out that the weeds were covering mounds of stone chippings for road building. The Hungarians had transported it there in 1913 or 1914, before the first world war! At least that was what the state secretary for transport said in 1940. The Romanians had left it there just as they'd found it.

Soon after part of the Székelyföld [*Szekler region*] had returned to Hungarian rule, during the time that István Horthy was president of MÁV, the railway between Szeretfalva [*Seretel*] and Déda was built, and a significant part of the road network was also repaired. Several people have already written about all this of course, and the general population could also find out about it from the newspapers and news broadcasts at the time. However, a good deal less was written about the altruistic activities of MANSZ [*Magyar Asszonyok Nemzeti Szövetsége—National Association of Hungarian Women*], which was led by István Horthy's wife. Because it was not just the president who maintained direct and human contacts with railway workers, but also his wife, who went with him to Kolozsvár, after which MANSZ extended its work to Transylvania.

MÁV was a large company with a network covering the whole country, and it had a very large number of employees. It is well known that even those working in the lowest-graded posts had to have a certain minimum knowledge, and so, depending on the kind of work they did, they received training at a lower or higher level. Those in higher posts valued railway staff who carried out their duties properly and honestly, no matter what position they held. Even the president of MÁV was considered a railwayman.

Let me recount just one of many stories which show how the president István Horthy acted when a man who had got into trouble needed his help.

There may be some people who still remember the case of the coupler Elek Pál.

It was a hot summer's day in August. The palace is very quiet. Only István Horthy and his wife were in residence, the Regent and his family were staying in Gödöllő. It was lunch time, and the two of them were sitting at the table. Suddenly the telephone rang: it was the porter.

"Gyuri, is that you?" asked Mr Angyal, recognising my voice.

"Yes. What is it?"

"There's a man here who wants to speak to you. He mentioned Mr István. Shall I ask someone to bring him up?" (Between ourselves we called the Regent's family by their first names.)

"Yes. I don't know who he is, but if he's asking for me by name then he must know me, or maybe I know him."

The guard on duty brought up a man who was wearing a raincoat even in the August midday heat, and worn-out shoes from which his toes stuck out. He greeted me politely and introduced himself: "I'm Elek Pál, a coupler at MÁV. We shunt trucks, crawl under carriages, and so on."

I looked at his ragged clothes. "Wait," I told him. I sent the guard away. I was just serving lunch, the door was open and our talk could be heard in the room.

"Who is it? Who has come?" asked my master.

"Elek Pál, sir. I don't know him. He says he's a railwayman. He would like to speak to you."

"Tell him everything's all right, he doesn't need to

191

thank me for anything." Turning to his wife, he said: "I'm very sorry for the unfortunate man. He was convicted of embezzlement and fraud. MÁV dismissed him and he served his sentence. Then there was a retrial and this time the court's verdict was different. His innocence was established: he hadn't committed any fraud or embezzlement. The real culprit received the punishment he deserved, and the court reinstated Elek Pál in his job. I ordered that he should immediately be re-employed in the place where he had worked before, and that his pay should be backdated. It's the least I could do. I'm very sorry for the poor man. But there's no need for him to come here and thank me."

"Sir, this man says he knows about the president's order, but that was two months ago and he hasn't been taken back," I said to my master as he sat at the table, eating his lunch.

István Horthy practically leapt from his chair. He hurried out and came face to face with Elek Pál, whom he had never seen in his life.

"What do you look like, you unfortunate man?" he said.

"Sir, my working clothes were taken away, and I haven't got any ordinary clothes. I was only given these rags out of charity."

"Wait," said my master. Striding over to his wardrobe, he took out a dark suit, gave it to him, and said: "Report to me in the office tomorrow morning at eight o'clock."

"They won't even let me in as far as the gate, sir," he answered.

"See to it that he gets in," the president of MÁV said to me. I often went in with him in the morning and he would give me my instructions at the office. I took Elek Pál out to the gate with his package, and said I'd see him the next morning at eight o'clock at the MÁV president's office.

The next morning we were at the president's office at a few minutes before eight o'clock. István Horthy did not allow himself to be late for work. And anyway it wouldn't have been proper to tell someone to be there at eight o'clock in the morning if he wasn't there or arrived late. István Horthy was very strict with himself. He was more tolerant with others, though when he gave a latecomer a look, that person would make every effort never to be late again. So anyway, Elek Pál was standing there in front of the gate, at a discreet distance. The president strode in, up the steps two at a time, and was up in his office in half a minute. Elek Pál was dressed as he had been the previous day. He couldn't put on the suit he'd been given: after all, a suit made for a man 197 cm tall won't alter itself just like that in half a day to fit a man 160–170 cm tall. The porter was watching the people going in, but before he could say a word, I loudly told him that this man was with me. He stared, but by the time he opened his mouth, we were inside. The president's secretary stared as well, wondering who that was with me. We greeted each other, then went straight into the president's office without being announced. The president of MÁV told his secretary to send for the manager whom he had told two months ago to deal with the matter. (He'd really dealt with it quickly!)

"This is Elek Pál. See to it that he starts work today, and that he reports to me tomorrow in uniform to tell me that he has taken up his duties and has received all his back pay."

This is typical of the way István Horthy acted. I have recounted it in detail as an example. There may still be some retired railwaymen from the Rákos shunting yard who remember the incident.

I don't want to glorify him: I've just described one case out of many to illustrate how my master valued ordinary workers, especially one who–in whatever position—was a "colleague" of his.

When he was elected Vice-Regent in 1942, he took his closest colleagues from MÁV with him. The head of his cabinet office, his secretary, the office manager, two typists and two assistants all came from MÁV: the Vice-Regent had a total staff of seven people.

BIOGRAPHICAL DETAILS OF VITÉZ ISTVÁN HORTHY DE NAGYBÁNYA

9 Dec. 1904	István Horthy born in Pola (Istria), son of Lieutenant Commander Miklós Horthy de Nagybánya and Magda Purgly de Joszas.
1904–1908	Lived with his parents and siblings in Pola and Constantinople (Istanbul).
1909–1914	Attended primary school in Vienna.
1914–1918	Attended lower four classes of secondary school in Baden. Learned French and English.
1918	Enrolled in the Fiume Royal Naval Academy, based in Braunau.
Spring 1919	Worked as a joiner's apprentice in Kenderes.
25 Nov. 1919	Enrolled in the 5th class of the Toldy Ferenc secondary school in Budapest.
1 June 1922	Passed a private examination on the combined material of the 7th and 8th classes; completed his studies at the Toldy Ferenc secondary school with outstanding results.
1922–1928	Studied and graduated in mechanical engineering at the József Nádor Technical University in Budapest.

1926	While still a university student, completed his year's voluntary military service as an officer designate with the rank of brevet bombardier.
1927	Qualified as a pilot.
1928–1929	Took part in a hunting expedition with Jenő Horthy and Kálmán Kittenberger in eastern and central Africa.
June–Sep 1929	Worked as a production engineer in the Weiss Manfred factory in Csepel, Budapest, in the department manufacturing Jupiter aircraft engines.
1 Oct. 1929	Became a reserve pilot officer.
Oct 1929–Oct 1930	Worked on the production line in Ford's Dearborn works, then as a design engineer in their Detroit works.
1930–1940	Chief engineer at MÁVAG, then deputy director, director, and also deputy managing director.
1 Jan. 1939	Became a reserve flying officer.
28 Feb. 1940	Engagement to Countess Ilona Edelsheim-Gyulai.
27 April 1940	Marriage to Countess Ilona Edelsheim-Gyulai.
1 June 1940	Appointed president of MÁV. (Hungarian State Railways)
17 Jan. 1941	Birth of István Horthy jr.
19 Feb. 1942	Elected Vice-Regent by the Parliament.
1 May 1942	Began military service with the 1st fighter division at Szolnok.
2 July 1942	Arrived at the Eastern Front.

6 Aug. 1942   Won a dogfight: shot down a Russian Rata.
20 Aug. 1942 Killed at 0507 hours when his plane crashed near the tactical reconnaissance airfield at Ilovskoye.

PHOTOGRAPHS

Number 1: Stephen Horthy at a polo match on Margaret Island in Budapest (1941). From the photograph collection of the Museum of Recent History (= LTMF) P. 88.220

Number 2: Setting off on his flight to Bombay in the Aradó 79 private plane (1939). From the collection of the widow of Stephen Horthy.

Number 3: A good-humoured account of the exciting flight. In the centre background: Count Gyula Károlyi and his wife, Paula Horthy (1939). LTMF P. 62.1993

Number 4: The president of MÁV at his desk. His black armband is a sign of mourning for his older sister Paula, who had recently died (1940). LTMF P. 85.1279

Number 5: Waving goodbye to the young couple leaving on their honeymoon from Budaörs airport (1940). LTMF P. 62.3809

Number 6: Mohamed Tahir Pasha, the president of the Egyptian flying club, takes his leave of Stephen Horthy at Almaza airport (1940). LTMF P. 68.288

Number 7: Election of the Vice-Regent in the Parliament (19 February 1942). LTMF P. 62.1985

Number 8: Leaving the Parliament building after taking the oath (19 February 1942). LTMF P. 62.3266

Number 9: Stephen Horthy after a sortie (August 1942).

Number 10: Stephen Horthy at the entrance to his tent (Ilovskoye, August 1942). From the collection of the widow of Stephen Horthy.

Number 11: Stephen Horthy at the front. On the right is General Gusztáv Jány, commander of the Hungarian 2nd Army; next to him is Major General Dezső László, commander of the 7th light division (July-August 1942). HMF P. 67.634

Number 12: Stephen Horthy in his V 421 Hawk fighter before a sortie (August 1942). HMF P. 67.412

Number 13: Return from a successful sortie (August 1942). From the collection of György Farkas.

Number 14: Stephen Horthy with Hungarian and German officers at the front. In the centre background is Colonel Gyula Kovács of the general staff, chief of staff of the Hungarian 2nd army; next to him is a German officer. HMF P. 67.394

Number 15: Flight Lt. Stephen Horthy briefs his squad (Ilovskoye, July 1942). LTMF P. 62.2000

Number 16: Stephen Horthy in Ilovskoye (August 1942). HMT P. 51.937/169

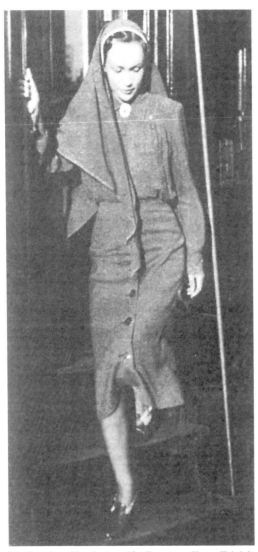

Number 17: Stephen Horthy's wife Countess Ilona Edelsheim-Gyulai, a Red Cross nurse and theatre sister (August 1942). From the collection of the widow of Stephen Horthy.

Number 18: Stephen Horthy and his wife at Kiev airport (18th August 1942). From the collection of the widow of Stephen Horthy.

Number 19: A Hawk fighter which overturned on landing. This also happened to Stephen Horthy on 10th July 1942. HMF slide no. 1718

Number 20: Vice-Regent Stephen Horthy welcoming his wife at Kiev station, accompanied by Hungarian and German officers (15th August 1942). LTMF P. 62.1996

Number 21: The last time they were together: Stephen Horthy and his wife in the car, ready to leave for Kiev airport (18th August 1942). Photograph by György Farkas.

Number 22: The wreckage of Stephen Horthy's crashed aeroplane at the tactical reconnaissance airfield at Ilovskoye (20th August 1942). HMF P. 67.584

Number 23: Memorial cross at the scene of the accident, in its final form (photo taken on 8th October 1942). HMF P. 67.586

Number 24: The coffin containing the remains of Stephen Horthy arriving at the railway station at Stary Oskol (21st August 1942). HMF P. 67.742

Number 25: Military parade in front of the Parliament building on the day of the funeral (27th August 1942). HMF P. 67.615

Number 26: Mourners leaving the Parliament building (27th August 1942). HMF N. 11.027

Number 27: The funeral procession leaves Kossuth Lajos square for the Nyugati station (27th August 1942). HMF P. 34.122

Number 28: After the burial at Kenderes (27th August 1942). HMF N. 10.988/Fkl.

INDEX

Álgyai-Hubert, Pál, a lecturer at the Technical
   University in Budapest. Formerly His Majesty's State
   Secretary for Transport, he is Vice-President of the
   Hungarian Transport Science Society   115, 118
Angyal   191
Antal, László, Editor   28
Antony, Endre, Lt.   100
Arany, János, poet   139
Balbo, Italo, Italian pilot   171
Baranyai, Elek, Captain   93, 105, 106, 109
Baross, Gábor   138
Bartha, Károly, Defense Minister   88
Berta, Gate Keeper   178, 179
Bezuk, Director   46
Bowden, Guy, Mrs   3
Bowden, Ilona, Widow of Stephen Horthy born
   Edelsheim-Gyulai, Ilona, Countess   5, 8, 171, 215
Bujtás, László, Publisher   100
Császár, Béla   100
Csukás, Kálmán   40, 45, 56, 66, 72, 84, 85
Edelsheim-Gyulai, Ilona, Countess, widow of Stephen
   Horthy, married, Bowden, Ilona   171
Egerszögi, József, Former Staff Sergeant   101
Elek, Lajos   29
Elek, Pál, Coupler   191, 192, 193
Ember, Sándor, Dr., Deputy in the Hungarian
   Parliament and President of the Horthy Miklós
   National Flying Foundation   159, 174

Eszláry, István, A chief government advisor, Deputy Director of MÁV, and former head of the Vice-Regent's secretariat *141*
Farkas, György, personal valet of Stephen Horthy *3, 5, 17, 78, 79, 90, 110, 112, 175, 212, 218*
Farouk, King *172*
Fehér, 2nd Lieutenant *73, 80*
Fenyo, Mario, D. *73, 80*
Ford *178, 180*
Fraknói, Miklós, Captain *100*
Gajzagó, István, Deputy *69*
Gémes, Sergeant *69*
Goebbels, Herman, Minister of Propaganda
Gyulai, István, 2nd Lieutenant *54*
Harmath, Ferenc, Staff Sergeant *25, 40, 41, 44, 54*
Háry, László *170*
Hermann, Clerk and Unit Leader *48*
Hess, Captain *63*
Hille, Jenő Oscar, Managing Director *179, 183*
Hitler, Adolf, Chancellar *12*
Hollán, Mária *8*
Horthy, István *11*
Horthy, Istvánné *3*
Horthy, Miklós *136, 141, 149, 153, 155, 172, 174*
Horthy, Stephen, Vice Regent of Hungary *1, 3, 4, 5, 11, 49, 50, 51, 52, 56, 57, 66, 67, 77, 79, 80, 84, 87, 88, 89, 93, 95, 96, 101, 105, 107, 109, 110, 111, 113, 115, 116, 117, 118, 120, 122, 123, 124, 125, 126, 127, 128, 129, 131, 134, 138, 139, 141, 142, 147, 149, 150, 151, 153, 154, 156, 157, 158, 159, 160, 161, 162, 163, 164, 166, 167, 168, 169, 170, 171, 172, 173, 174, 177, 178, 179, 180, 181, 182, 183, 184, 185, 186, 189, 190, 191, 192, 193, 195, 203, 204, 205, 207, 209, 210, 211, 213, 214, 215, 217, 218, 219*
Horthy, Stephen, widow *5, 8*

Horváth, Sándor   54
Imrédy, Kálmán, Dr Kálmán Imrédy de Omorovicza, is President of the Board of MÁV, and Vice-president of the Hungarian Transport Science Society   *131, 139*
Jagov, von Dietrich, German Ambassador   *12*
Jány, Gusztáv, General   *50, 53, 85, 211*
Kállay, Miklós, Prime Minister   *88*
Károlyi, Gyula, Count   *173*
Kern, Irma   *184*
Kitzinger, General   *12*
Kovács, Attila, Photographer   *5*
Kovács, Gyula, Colonel   *213*
Laboczffy, Rezső   *153, 158*
Láner, Kornél, President of MÁV   *182, 189*
László, Dezső   *211*
Latinovits, Margit   *181*
Magyar, Sándor   *157*
Maléter, Jenő   *129, 139, 147, 151, 159, 174*
Markotay-Velsz, Jenő, a chief government advisor and Managing Director of the Hungarian State Iron, Steel and Machine Works (MÁVAG)   *118, 119, 129, 177*
Mészáros, Rafael, Corporal   *85, 90, 100*
Mocsáry, Captain   *63*
Nemeslaki, Zoltán, Sergeant   *66, 73, 93*
Német, György, Officer designate, war correspondent   *80*
Németh, József, General   *63*
Nilsen, Anna, Translator of this book   *2, 4, 8, 11*
Ortutay, Tivadar, Reserve 2nd Lieutenant, Stephen Horthy's personal interpreter   *11, 40, 61*
Palotai, László, Lieutenant   *100*
Panczel Pilot officer   *57*
Péterffy, Sergeant   *67, 68*
Pintér, László, Photographer   *5*
Pista   *149*

Pohly, Colonel   60
Polgár, Béla, Deputy   69
Rákosi, Béla, Lieutenant General   58
Rátvay, Captain   70
Rédey, George, Publisher   8
Ribbentrop, Foreign Minister   13
Romer, Pilot, Officer   56
Schell, Baron   61
Segesváry, György, Hungarian Royal Trade and Transport Ministry   149, 151
St. László   123, 143
St. Stephen   163
Szabó, Gyula, Pilot, Officer   97, 101, 108
Szabó, László, Major General   25, 42, 51, 53, 61, 62, 67, 78, 111
Szabó, Mátyás, Captain   25, 28
Széchényi, István   137, 138, 139
Szentgyörgyi, Sergeant   66
Szidike, Wife of György Farkas   19, 58
Tahir, Mohamed, President of the Egyptian flying club   207
Takács   180
Takács, Andor, György Farkas's brother-in-law   21, 68, 69, 180
Teleki, Pál, Count   135
Tornyi, Victor, Sergant   71
Tost, Gyula, Major   57, 58
Wágner, Károly, Acting Pilot Officer   93, 96, 97, 105, 106, 109
Wulff, Olaf   118, 121, 139, 147, 151, 158, 174
Zichy, Nándor, Count   43, 63

CONTENTS

WIDOW OF STEPHEN HORTHY:
IT MUST BE TOLD   9

GYÖRGY FARKAS: WAR DIARY   17

GYÖRGY NÉMET: AN ORPHANED CAMP   75

GYÖRGY FARKAS: FIFTY YEARS ON   81

WITNESSES RECALL THE EVENTS OF
50 YEARS AGO   91

FORMER ACTING PILOT,
OFFICER KÁROLY WÁGNER   93

AN UNUSUAL WITNESS:
FORMER CORPORAL RAFAEL MÉSZÁROS   99

THE OBSERVATIONS OF FORMER STAFF
SERGEANT JÓZSEF EGERSZÖGI   101

DOCUMENTS   103

REMEMBERING FLIGHT LT. STEPHEN HORTHY:
BY THOSE WHO KNEW HIM WELL   113

PÁL ÁLGYAI-HUBERT: THE EMBODIMENT OF
A MODERN ENGINEER   115

JENŐ MARKOTAY-VELSZ:
THE DEPUTY MANAGING DIRECTOR
OF THE STATE IRON WORKS   *119*

KÁLMÁN IMRÉDY:
ISTVÁN HORTHY AS PRESIDENT
OF THE STATE RAILWAYS   *131*

ISTVÁN ESZLÁRY:
IN THE PRESIDENT'S OFFICE   *141*

GYÖRGY SEGESVÁRY:
THE FIRST VOLUNTEER PILOT   *149*

REZSŐ LABORCZFFY:
ISTVÁN HORTHY'S ACHIEVEMENTS
IN CIVILIAN AVIATION   *153*

SÁNDOR EMBER:
A FEW BRUSHSTROKES OF A PORTRAIT
OF ISTVÁN HORTHY AS A PILOT   *159*

GYÖRGY (GYURI) FARKAS:
MY MASTER—AS I SAW HIM   *175*
AT MÁVAG   *177*
TO INDIA IN A PRIVATE PLANE   *183*
AT THE HEAD OF THE STATE RAILWAYS   *189*

BIOGRAPHICAL DETAILS OF
VITÉZ ISTVÁN HORTHY DE NAGYBÁNYA   *195*

PHOTOGRAPHS   *201*

INDEX OF NAMES   *223*

CONTENTS   *229*

LIST OF ILLUSZTRATION   *233*

LIST OF ILLUSTRATION

Number 1: Stephen Horthy at a polo match on Margaret Island in Budapest (1941). From the photograph collection of the Museum of Recent History (= LTMF) P. 88.220

Number 2: Setting off on his flight to Bombay in the Aradó 79 private plane (1939). From the collection of the widow of Stephen Horthy.

Number 3: A good-humoured account of the exciting flight. In the centre background: Count Gyula Károlyi and his wife, Paula Horthy (1939). LTMF P. 62.1993

Number 5: Waving goodbye to the young couple leaving on their honeymoon from Budaörs airport (1940). LTMF P. 62.3809

Number 4: The president of MÁV at his desk. His black armband is a sign of mourning for his older sister Paula, who had recently died (1940). LTMF P. 85.1279

Number 6: Mohamed Tahir Pasha, the president of the Egyptian flying club, takes his leave of Stephen Horthy at Almaza airport (1940). LTMF P. 68.288

Number 7: Election of the Vice-Regent in the Parliament (19 February 1942). LTMF P. 62.1985

Number 8: Leaving the Parliament building after taking the oath (19 February 1942). LTMF P. 62.3266

Number 9: Stephen Horthy after a sortie (August 1942).

Number 10: Stephen Horthy at the entrance to his tent (Ilovskoye, August 1942). From the collection of the widow of Stephen Horthy.

Number 11: Stephen Horthy at the front. On the right is General Gusztáv Jány, commander of the Hungarian 2nd Army; next to him is Major General Dezső László, commander of the 7th light division (July-August 1942). HMF P. 67.634

Number 12: Stephen Horthy in his V 421 Hawk fighter before a sortie (August 1942). HMF P. 67.412

Number 13: Return from a successful sortie (August 1942). From the collection of György Farkas.

Number 14: Stephen Horthy with Hungarian and German officers at the front. In the centre background is Colonel Gyula Kovács of the general staff, chief of staff of the Hungarian 2nd army; next to him is a German officer. HMF P. 67.394

Number 15: Flight Lt. Stephen Horthy briefs his squad (Ilovskoye, July 1942). LTMF P. 62.2000

Number 16: Stephen Horthy in Ilovskoye (August 1942). HMT P. 51.937/169

Number 17: Stephen Horthy's wife Countess Ilona Edelsheim-Gyulai, a Red Cross nurse and theatre sister (August 1942). From the collection of the widow of Stephen Horthy.

Number 18: Stephen Horthy and his wife at Kiev airport (18th August 1942). From the collection of the widow of Stephen Horthy.

Number 19: A Hawk fighter which overturned on landing. This also happened to Stephen Horthy on 10th July 1942. HMF slide no. 1718

Number 20: Vice-Regent Stephen Horthy welcoming his wife at Kiev station, accompanied by Hungarian and German officers (15th August 1942). LTMF P. 62.1996

Number 21: The last time they were together: Stephen Horthy and his wife in the car, ready to leave for Kiev airport (18th August 1942). Photograph by György Farkas.

Number 22: The wreckage of Stephen Horthy's crashed aeroplane at the tactical reconnaissance airfield at Ilovskoye (20th August 1942). HMF P. 67.584

Number 23: Memorial cross at the scene of the accident, in its final form (photo taken on 8th October 1942). HMF P. 67.586

Number 24: The coffin containing the remains of Stephen Horthy arriving at the railway station at Stary Oskol (21st August 1942). HMF P. 67.742

Number 25: Military parade in front of the Parliament building on the day of the funeral (27th August 1942). HMF P. 67.615

Number 26: Mourners leaving the Parliament building (27th August 1942). HMF N. 11.027

Number 27: The funeral procession leaves Kossuth Lajos square for the Nyugati station (27th August 1942). HMF P. 34.122

Number 28: After the burial at Kenderes (27th August 1942). HMF N. 10.988/Fkl.